HBR Guide to
Getting the Mentoring You Need

Harvard Business Review Guides

Arm yourself with the advice you need to succeed on the job, from the most trusted brand in business. Packed with how-to essentials from leading experts, the HBR Guides provide smart answers to your most pressing work challenges.

The titles include:

HBR Guide to Better Business Writing

HBR Guide to Finance Basics for Managers

HBR Guide to Getting the Mentoring You Need

HBR Guide to Getting the Right Job

HBR Guide to Getting the Right Work Done

HBR Guide to Giving Effective Feedback

HBR Guide to Making Every Meeting Matter

HBR Guide to Managing Stress at Work

HBR Guide to Managing Up and Across

HBR Guide to Persuasive Presentations

HBR Guide to Project Management

HBR Guide to
Getting the Mentoring You Need

HARVARD BUSINESS REVIEW PRESS

Boston, Massachusetts

The web addresses referenced in this book were live and correct at the time of the book's publication but may be subject to change.

Library of Congress Cataloging-in-Publication Data

HBR guide to getting the mentoring you need.
     pages cm
   ISBN 978-1-4221-9600-7 (alk. paper)
   1. Mentoring in business.   2. Career development.   I. Harvard business review.
   HF5385.H34 2014
   650.14—dc23
                                            2013032976

ISBN: 9781422196007
eISBN: 9781422197493

The paper used in this publication meets the requirements of the American National Standard for Permanence of Paper for Publications and Documents in Libraries and Archives Z39.48–1992.

What You'll Learn

Stuck in a career rut? Maybe you're itching to broaden your skills and take on new challenges. Or perhaps you're eyeing a management role a level or two up.

So how do you grow and advance professionally? Not by waiting for senior managers to notice you and "bring you along." You'll be sorely disappointed by how long that takes, if it ever happens.

The key is effective mentoring—and it's up to *you* to go get it. Done right, mentoring is one of the most powerful, efficient tools for learning and moving up. But to reap those rewards, you need to pursue them with rigor and commitment. This guide will show you how.

You'll get better at:

- Deciding which skills to sharpen

- Finding new ways to shine in your organization

- Setting clear, realistic development goals

- Attracting influential sponsors

- Forging strong bonds with your mentors

- Giving *back* to them

- Accepting and using feedback

- Gauging your progress

- Building a diverse "developmental network"

- Learning from executives, peers, and protégés

Contents

Contents

Section 3: GROWTH AND ADVANCEMENT

Introduction

Taking Charge of Your Career

by Tamara Erickson

Think of the most valuable insights you've gained about work and life. Chances are, those gems came to you through some form of mentoring, not from textbooks or classroom lectures. People with the experience, knowledge, skills, or perspective you seek have shared their wisdom with you, maybe even helped you put it to use.

Mentoring is indispensable to learning throughout our careers, not just while we're wet behind the ears. It's how we identify and fill critical gaps we'd struggle to address on our own. A good mentor is part diagnostician, assessing what's going on with you now, and part guide, connecting you with the advice, ideas, people, and resources you need to grow and move ahead.

That kind of support is essential these days, since career paths are anything but simple and straightforward. You now have more options than you know what to do with. And even if you do have a clear sense of direction, you probably face organizational and personal hurdles. These factors complicate matters further:

- **Shifting roles.** Your developmental needs change as you move from mastering *content* (producing the goods or services your company sells) to shaping *context* (setting the stage for other contributors to thrive). Generally, roles shift from content to context as you move up in an organization—but even that is changing as traditional, hierarchical structures break down. Many "senior" roles involve equal parts strategy and execution, and many "junior" folks get involved in high-level discussions about company values and goals. So it can be hard to sort out exactly which skills you need to build at what time. Mentors bring a fresh perspective, combined with a vested interest in your success— they work with you to identify the keys to your progress and modify your behavior appropriately.

- **Calibrating career potential.** Sooner or later, most of us weigh our career expectations against our fundamental capabilities and passions, the time and energy we want to invest in our work, and the demands imposed by our lives outside work. That's hard to do in isolation. Again, mentors can help you assess where you are and figure out next steps. Mentoring does not always have to be about climbing—it can involve finding peace with the life you're leading, making the most of your choices, or carving out a new niche.

As critical as they are, good mentors almost never come your way unbidden. Waiting for others to reach out to you, or for your employer to play matchmaker, rarely pans out—certainly not with the frequency and commitment that you need and your career deserves. Although many companies recognize that mentoring leads to bench strength for them, not just opportunities for you, those that actually provide it tend to do so in old-school ways, through top-down, highly managed, overly scheduled "arranged marriages" between organizational veterans and newbies. Programs that assign senior individuals to junior counterparts—of course, in a good-faith effort to match interests and personalities—are minimally effective because they're not tailored enough. They also force relationships instead of allowing them to develop organically, over time, through mutual trust and respect. And the follow-up is often spotty. Some company-assigned mentors take their mentees out to lunch once and then check that responsibility off their "to do" list.

The bottom line: Even if you participate in a formal mentoring program, it's up to you to find the right people to work with, form strong relationships with them, tap them when you need them the most, and—just as important—return the favor. This guide will help you do all that.

For starters, Sylvia Ann Hewlett and her coauthors explain in the opening chapter how you'll benefit from dedicated *sponsors*—mentors who go above and beyond to provide advocacy, resources, and tactical support so you'll prosper in the organization. (Traditional mentors offer guidance and emotional support, but they're not as inclined as sponsors to stand up for you or call in favors for you.) Use the information in the first section of this guide to consider what kinds of mentoring will best serve your needs. You'll also discover different, unexpected sources of mentoring that others have found valuable.

Then, as you're reading the second section, you'll step back and think more deeply about your current situation and where you want to go. For example, Harvard Business School management professor Robert S. Kaplan advises taking a very personal look at what success means to you and offers thoughtful guidance on how to get there. Other expert authors wrestle with tough issues like how to make yourself indispensable at work and why you didn't get the promotion you were hoping for.

Finally, in the third section, you'll get practical counsel on finding the right types of mentors, defining your goals and expectations, building relationships, establishing a give-and-take dynamic, networking effectively—in short, making mentoring *work for you*. You'll also find tips expressly for Millennials and Gen Xers, and ways to learn meaningfully from your own protégés.

At this point in your career, you may discover that you don't enjoy your work and need help charting a better course. Or you might find your work engaging but still feel stuck or confused about where you're headed in the future. Or you may simply want to change the intensity of your work—to do less or do more. Working closely and deliberately with a mentor, you can meet challenges like these by playing to your strengths, building the *right* skills, understanding your role in greater depth, learning to manage up, expanding your career options through networking, and making smart work/life trade-offs.

All this takes time and discipline—but it's well worth the investment.

Tamara Erickson works with corporations to more effectively engage the changing workforce. She is the author of a trilogy of books on the generations: *Retire Retirement, Plugged In,* and *What's Next, Gen X?* (Harvard Business Review Press, 2008, 2008, and 2010). She was named one of the 50 leading management thinkers in 2009 and 2011 by Thinkers50.

Section 1
What Good Mentoring Looks Like

Chapter 1
The Relationship You Need to Get Right

by Sylvia Ann Hewlett, Melinda Marshall, and Laura Sherbin

Katharine, a senior HR executive at a global financial services firm, takes pride in developing rising stars. After a vice president on one of her teams consistently impressed her, she recommended him for a more challenging role in another part of the company. Months later Katharine heard through the grapevine that he was struggling in the job. She asked to meet with him. "You know we're in this together, right?" she said. "I put my reputation on the line, but I have no idea how you're performing and

Reprinted from *Harvard Business Review*, October 2011 (product #R1110K)

whether you need help or air cover." He promised to keep her in the loop, but communication dropped off again. Katharine realized that his commitment to the firm, and to her, had waned. She met with him once more and told him she could no longer be his sponsor.

When Maria, a manager at a U.S. health care firm, was invited to join a mentoring program for high-potential women, she anticipated getting guidance that would help her advance. But her assigned mentor, a physician and vice president, took little interest in Maria's career; instead she lectured to the group about her own path and gave direct advice only to the participants who were also MDs. In the end Maria turned to existing allies for career support. "Not everyone in leadership knows how to be an advocate," she reflects.

In 2003 Mark McLane, an openly gay innovation consultant at Whirlpool, was asked to serve on the company's diversity council, headed by then-COO Jeff Fettig. He excelled at the work and in 2004 sought an appointment to southwest Michigan's Council for World Class Communities, a nonprofit that furthers economic and social growth in the largely African-American community of Benton Harbor, Michigan, where the company is headquartered. Fettig supported his bid and also persuaded CEO David Whitwam to make McLane Whirlpool's director of diversity, enabling him to be the council's executive-on-loan. That year Fettig moved up to the CEO job and gave his protégé a new mission: to ensure gender balance among senior managers globally. McLane set four-year goals and aligned Whirlpool's recruiting strategy accordingly. "Mark not only grasped our vision for key areas of the company, he played a critical role in implementing it," Fettig says.

McLane also demonstrated his allegiance to Fettig outside the office. The CEO is a trustee of the local Boys and Girls Club, a nonprofit he sees as key to making Benton Harbor a "world-class community" that might have greater appeal to Whirlpool recruits and be more likely to yield local talent. McLane joined the board and, with Fettig's coaching, became president after six months. He instituted reforms that turned the organization's $125,000 deficit into a $500,000 reserve and nearly doubled its membership within a year. "If someone believes in you and gives you an opportunity, it is incumbent upon you to go the extra mile," he observes.

The Dynamics of Sponsorship

As the earlier examples show, the relationship between sponsor and protégé works best when it helps *both* parties. Katharine, who requested anonymity to protect her firm's reputation, cut ties with her former vice president because he failed to demonstrate basic responsiveness, let alone deliver the standout proactive effort she'd expected. Maria, who asked for anonymity because she still works with the physician once assigned to mentor her, found that the older woman lacked a grasp of the give-and-take intrinsic to effective guidance. By contrast, Fettig and McLane worked together on the twin goals of hitting Whirlpool's business targets and enhancing their reputations as leaders in the community.

Sponsorship can help catapult junior talent into top management while also greatly expanding the reach and impact of senior leadership—but only when both sponsor and protégé recognize that it's a mutually beneficial alliance, a truly two-way street.

Our recent research bears this out. We conducted three national surveys of nearly 4,000 professionals in large corporations, held focus groups with more than 60 vice presidents and senior vice presidents, and interviewed nearly 20 *Fortune* 500 executives. The best sponsors, we found, go beyond mentoring. They offer not just guidance but also advocacy, not just vision but also the tactical means of realizing it. They place bets on outstanding junior colleagues and call in favors for them. The most successful protégés, for their part, recognize that sponsorship must be earned with performance and loyalty—not just once but continually.

We repeatedly heard CEOs and top managers say that they wouldn't be where they are without strong sponsors *and* loyal protégés. One *Fortune* 500 CEO gave a powerful illustration. When interviewing candidates for senior positions, he always asks them, "How many people do you have in your pocket? If I asked you to pull off something impossible that involved liaising across seven geographies and five functions, who owes you one and could help you do it?" He told us, "I'm not interested in anyone who doesn't have deep pockets."

Ensuring that you have sponsors is a lifelong project no matter what your position. As she neared retirement age, a senior partner at Ernst & Young belatedly recognized that she hadn't "refreshed" her pool of sponsors. "I had always looked forward to a second career as a board director, but I'm realizing that being selected for a board seat is all about sponsorship," she says. "You can't apply for these positions; you've got to be tapped." Nor is it ever too early for a junior executive to start cultivating protégés. Kris Urbauer, the manager of veterans' initiatives at GE, acknowledged that to achieve CEO Jeffrey Immelt's goal of making the company an appealing employer for returning vets, she would have to develop a posse of high-performing subordinates. "With all eyes on me to deliver, I'm going to need some dedicated help," she told us.

Our first exploration of sponsorship, a 2011 HBR special report titled "The Sponsor Effect," revealed the impact a sponsor can have on virtually every aspect of an employee's career, boosting the ability to ask for and get raises and promotions and find satisfaction at work. Yet relatively few of the employees we surveyed—19% of men and 13% of women—reported having a sponsor. The use of a sponsor as a career lever is sometimes poorly understood, other times perceived as rife with risk. And corporate initiatives designed to jump-start sponsorships have had at best mixed results. Leaders can't lobby convincingly for up-and-comers they don't know, and junior employees paired with sponsors don't see what they can contribute or can't deliver it.

Seeking to better understand these relationships, we launched a second round of research. Our initiative, Sponsor Effect 2.0, enabled us to map the quid pro quo: how protégés can attract, sustain, and deploy sponsors to progress in their careers, and how sponsors can use the dynamic to extend their reach, expand their skills, build networks, and demonstrate leadership.

The Sponsor's Role

What exactly does a sponsor do? According to our research, it boils down to two things: putting one's reputation on the line for a protégé and taking responsibility for his or her promotion. A good sponsor will groom you to audition for a key part in a prominent production, nudge the director to choose you, and coach you on your performance. While you're onstage, she'll train a spotlight on you so that everyone takes note of your abilities and potential. Should you stumble, or should the audience turn hostile, she'll come to your aid (at least the first time). After all, "protégé" means "one who's protected."

When we asked managers what they hoped for in a sponsor, 74% said they want a sponsor to provide honest feedback, specifically by suggesting ways for the protégé to narrow gaps in skills and experience. Other frequent responses included "provide feedback on how to look and act like a leader" (59%), "provide opportunities for visibility internally" (49%), "help me define career goals" (44%), and "be willing to defend me" (41%).

The degree to which a sponsor will come to the rescue of a protégé varies considerably, however. A Siemens executive told us her sponsorship has to be clearly merited lest it look like favoritism. "If you screw up, I may step in, but if you continue not to thrive, I'll have to step away," she says. At the law firm White & Case, by contrast, partner and tax attorney Jim Hayden supported his protégé Someera Khokhar repeatedly. When Khokhar had a conflict with another partner, Hayden intervened to mend fences. When long-term clients demurred at liaising primarily with an associate, Hayden vouched for Khokhar's expertise. In subtle and overt ways he ensured that she could thrive—which indeed she did, eventually making partner. "Every time I needed something, he made it happen, whether by his presence or his influence," Khokhar recalls.

The Protégé's Part

What protégés should do for their sponsors is less well understood. Our survey indicated that the top two imperatives are demonstrating trust and showing loyalty. (Some 61% agreed with the former idea and 49% agreed with the latter one.) When we asked potential sponsors, 62% said protégés should "assume responsibility and be self-directed," 39% said they should "deliver 110%," and 34% said they should "offer skill sets and bring a perspective different than mine." One respondent summed it up this way: "A protégé who doesn't do everything in her power to make her sponsor look smart for backing her is wasting the sponsor's time."

Ed Gadsden, the chief diversity officer at Pfizer, emphasizes that a protégé should keep her sponsor apprised of critical developments, conversations that might be off his radar, and constituencies outside his circle. He recalls a conversation with his sponsor, the late legal scholar and federal judge Leon Higginbotham. Early on Gadsden asked Higginbotham what he got out of the relationship. Higginbotham replied, "You're nothing like me. The people you're around, the things you see, what you're

MENTORS AND SPONSORS: HOW THEY DIFFER

Companies need to make a sharper distinction between mentoring and sponsorship. Mentors offer "psychosocial" support for personal and professional development, plus career help that includes advice and coaching, as Boston University's Kathy Kram explains in her pioneering research. Only sponsors actively advocate for advancement.

"Classical mentoring" (ideal but rare) combines psychosocial and career support. Usually, though, workers get one or the other—or if they get both, it's from different sources. Analysis of hundreds of studies shows that people derive more satisfaction from mentoring but need sponsorship. Without sponsorship, a person is likely to be overlooked for promotion, regardless of his or her competence and performance—particularly at midcareer and beyond, when competition for promotions increases.

hearing—you provide a perspective I wouldn't otherwise have." Today Gadsden appreciates this quality in his own protégés.

Several successful protégés spoke of achieving their sponsor's vision (recall Mark McLane). At a large government contractor, one team leader, a former member of the military, described a boss whose big-picture goals required great tactical expertise. "I'd see where he wanted to go, and I didn't say 'That's never going to work' but rather 'Yes, sir!'" he told us. "I found solutions—and he

Mentors	Sponsors
• Can sit at any level in the hierarchy	• Must be senior managers with influence
• Provide emotional support, feedback on how to improve, and other advice	• Give protégés exposure to other executives who may help their careers
• Serve as role models	• Make sure their people are considered for promising opportunities and challenging assignments
• Help mentees learn to navigate corporate politics	
• Strive to increase mentees' sense of competence and self-worth	• Protect their protégés from negative publicity or damaging contact with senior executives
• Focus on mentees' personal and professional development	• Fight to get their people promoted

Excerpted from *Harvard Business Review*, September 2010 (product #R1009F)

appreciated that. Together we really drove results and fast-tracked both our careers."

Finding Each Other

Most sponsors cultivate protégés not from self-serving motives but because it's "the right thing to do" and can be a gratifying experience. "Paying it forward is my way of paying back the people who helped me get where I am to-day," says Annmarie Neal, the chief talent officer at Cisco.

Leaders will give their time, attention, and relation-ship capital only to people who perform exceptionally well. Katharine's vice president caught her attention, she told us, because he was "the kind of guy you could put in a room and he'd come up with that big idea." Sponsors also get behind those who are hungry for backing. Cyn-thia Rivera, a senior diversity specialist at Freddie Mac, notes, "They've got to show me they're going to make the most of what I have to give." Finally, while many spon-sors seek protégés who balance their own strengths and weaknesses, they also tend to support people with similar values, mind-sets, or backgrounds. "My race and gender often form the basis for my affinity, because there are so few female multicultural leaders in tech," says Rosalind Hudnell, the chief diversity officer at Intel. "I see myself in them and in the challenges they'll face, which allows me to help them in ways others might not be able to."

Junior executives should be just as selective when seeking sponsors, and they should take a proactive ap-proach. One IT professional highlights a common mis-take. "I was great at building business and had tons of cheerleaders, but I had that typical Asian keep-your-head-down-and-you'll-get-taken-care-of mind-set," he recalls. "My boss had to take me aside and tell me that if I didn't actively cultivate her as my sponsor, I would never progress beyond senior associate."

The most successful protégés are not content with one sponsor. Throughout their careers they scan the horizon for leaders who either embody their values (the quality most sought by 45% of the protégés we polled) or value their strengths (43%). They target leaders whose style they can complement—bringing tactical follow-through skills to visionaries or offering pushback to collaborators. They target leaders they think could benefit from their networks as well as their expertise.

And they routinely *ask* for career guidance, feedback, and stretch assignments. A vice president with 26 years of experience remembers consistently approaching her bosses for more responsibility. "Sponsors cannot be clairvoyant," she explains. "If you want to grow in the organization, then spell out how—and the introductions or team postings will follow."

Cynthia Rivera recalls that early in her career she asked for an appointment with the executive vice president; when his assistant pressed to know her business, she said it was a personal matter. During the meeting she laid out her career history and desired trajectory, soliciting feedback on the skills and experience she might need. "Ask for input, not a job," she recommends. "You don't want to go in there waving a résumé." The strategy paid off: By the end of the meeting she had won a sponsor.

Women seem particularly reluctant to be so proactive. "They don't want to have to toot their own horn," explains Subha Barry, a senior vice president at Freddie Mac. During a previous job at Merrill Lynch she found an alternate strategy. She asked three female colleagues, all reporting to different executives, to meet monthly over lunch to discuss one another's work. That way they could knowledgeably promote the others to those in their own circles. "When women talk about each other, we can be quite eloquent," Barry observes. "So I might say to my boss in response to a problem he was airing, 'This is something my colleague Lisa's been working on; she's got some great ideas. You need to talk to her.'" The strategy was remarkably effective, gaining Barry and her lunchmates C-level positions within and outside the firm.

Respondents offered several additional sponsor-winning tactics. Chief among them was "leading with a yes": voicing enthusiasm when offered a challenging assignment. (If you have reservations, don't air them right away.) Others included bringing in new business, keeping potential sponsors "in the know," and developing a product or service on their behalf.

Maintaining the Relationship

Winning a sponsor is just the beginning. The relationship must be consistently nurtured and periodically refreshed—tasks that fall to the junior player. Successful protégés understand that sustaining sponsorship looks a lot like earning it: meeting deadlines, exceeding targets, and proving you will advance the larger mission. They recognize the importance of regular meetings, whether face-to-face or by phone or e-mail. They know to look for opportunities to forge bonds. And they find ways to support a sponsor's passion or help build his or her legacy outside the organization.

Protégés can also strengthen their relationships with sponsors by becoming sponsors themselves, because harnessing and growing talent is arguably the best demonstration of leadership ability. "Tiger" Tyagarajan, the CEO of Genpact, is a case in point. During the 17 years when he was the protégé of then-CEO Pramod Bhasin, he distinguished himself by building highly effective teams from scratch. "I had to hire people with background and depth and then sell them a vision, because I was putting them into what looked like a small job and making it their business to grow it," he recalls. "My ability to attract big people, get them excited, and keep them excited was one of the main drivers of my career."

Mark McLane is now the director of diversity and inclusion at Booz Allen Hamilton and is mindful of cultivating his own protégés. He recently lobbied for a team member's advancement, and that associate is returning the favor, ensuring that what's near and dear to McLane gets communicated across divisions. "He's promoting not just the percentages I've driven but the cultural changes I've effected," McLane says. "I'll continue to expend capital on him because he's taking my mission forward in ways neither of us could have foreseen."

Sylvia Ann Hewlett is the founding president of the Center for Work-Life Policy and SA Hewlett Associates and the chair of the Hidden Brain Drain, a task force of 67 global companies. **Melinda Marshall** is a senior fellow at CWLP, and **Laura Sherbin** is a senior vice president and the director of research there.

Chapter 2
Mentoring in All Its Shapes and Sizes

by Amy Gallo

When you think of mentoring, do you envision a sage executive counseling a junior upstart for years and years? It doesn't usually work that way anymore. Over the past few decades, mentoring has evolved into guidance and support from all kinds of sources—yet our collective thinking about it hasn't changed with the times. Here's a roundup of four dated but persistent myths you'll need to push past to grow and advance in your career.

Myth #1: You have to find one perfect mentor

It's actually rare to get through your career with only one mentor; most people today have several. So it makes sense that Boston University management professor

Adapted from content posted on hbr.org on February 1, 2011

Kathy Kram prefers the term *developmental network:* "It's that handful of people you can go to for advice and can trust to have your best interests in mind," she says. Your developmental network can be as large or small as you want and may include people you know on a personal level, such as friends and family members. Some of the key benefits of having more than one mentor within close reach: You can get a variety of perspectives on a challenge you're facing, you'll have ready access to people with different areas of expertise, and you're less likely to wear people out if you have more than one mentor to answer questions and respond to ideas.

Consider how Soki Choi, a mobile app developer whose start-up was acquired, sought career mentoring from several people in her developmental network when she was considering next steps: Should she take a job with another telecom company, start a new business, or switch fields and pursue a degree in medical research, as she'd always wanted to do? For guidance, she turned to Ewa Ställdal, the CEO of a major medical research foundation, who connected Choi with others in the field so she could do her homework; former Ericsson CEO Björn Svedberg, who urged her to pursue her dreams as he wished he had done; and Choi's friend Martin Lorentzon, who'd made a similarly dramatic career change of his own. All those perspectives shaped her decision to get a medical PhD at the Karolinska Institute rather than accept one of the many telecom job offers that came her way.

Myth #2: Mentoring is always a formal long-term relationship

Because we change jobs and careers more often than we used to, a long-term advising relationship may not be realistic or necessary. Think of mentoring as something you tap when you need it. "Mentoring can be a one-hour session. We don't have to escalate it to a six-month or yearlong event," says Karie Willyerd, cofounder of the executive development firm Future Workplace. "You don't need to wait until you have some big thing in your career," adds Jeanne Meister, Willyerd's fellow Future Workplace cofounder. These days, Meister says, mentoring is often "more like Twitter and less like a psychotherapy session."

Of course, the guidance may be richer and more relevant if it comes from someone who knows you well and understands your goals. You still need to build other relationships, though, so you'll have connections in place when you require advice that people closer to you can't provide. Occasionally, you may want to turn to someone who doesn't know you at all to get one-off counsel from an outsider's point of view.

Myth #3: Mentoring is only for junior people

"We used to think it was people at early stages of their career who needed mentoring, those just out of MBA programs," says Kram. "Now we understand that people at every stage benefit from this kind of assistance." Sometimes, as Meister and Willyerd point out in *The 2020 Workplace,* it even makes sense to flip the traditional

---

Coaching versus mentoring

Your coach should . . .	Your mentor should . . .
Focus on performance improvement or skill development	Provide career guidance, protection, and (ideally) sponsorship within the organization
Work with you to set clear, performance-based goals you can realistically meet in a short amount of time	Invite exploration and discovery, often over a longer period of time
Ask questions that prompt you to discover your own solutions	Model, teach, advise, motivate, and inspire

Adapted from *The Center for Creative Leadership Handbook of Leadership Development* (Jossey-Bass, 2010).

---

roles and have a junior colleague advising a senior one on things like new technology. No matter where the teaching comes from, if it's smart and useful, we need to be receptive to it.

That may not come naturally if you think you're already at the top of your game, as Stephen Wachter did after two decades in the recruiting business. When he founded the firm Osprey One, he landed some of the largest clients in Silicon Valley, including Google, Yahoo, and Facebook. Two years ago, his view of himself changed when he sat next to Susan Robertson, a leadership development consultant, on a plane headed to the East Coast. When they started talking about what they did, Wachter proudly shared his successes—and Robertson asked him, "So, what's your next step?" The question blew him away. He thought he simply had to keep doing what he was doing. In talking to Robertson, though, Wachter realized he had room to grow in how he interacted with his clients. He also saw that if he stopped developing, the industry would grow without him and pass him by.

Wachter and Robertson have stayed in touch and continue to have a mentoring relationship. They have regularly scheduled conversations in which Robertson helps him think through challenges he's facing and forces him to reflect on who he is and how he is with others. Because she holds him accountable for his own development, he doesn't get complacent: "The danger," he now understands, "is when you think you've got it all figured out."

Myth #4: Mentoring is something more experienced people do out of the goodness of their hearts

Though mentors can get a lot of satisfaction from helping people develop and learn, the relationship should be useful to both parties. Before you reach out to a mentor, think about what you have to offer as a mentee: Can you provide a unique perspective on the organization? Do you bring valuable information that might help your mentor succeed in his job? Whatever it is, be clear with your prospective adviser about what's in it for him. This does not have to be a direct barter. Even the promise of future help, if and when it's needed, may persuade a mentor to share his time and energy with you.

Now that you have a better understanding of what mentoring can be, do you need it? "The place to start is with self-assessment, to find out what are the challenges in front of you . . . and why," says Kram. "Then ask yourself, do you have the relational resources to handle those challenges?" If the answer is no, it may be time to seek out one mentor or several, junior or senior. The key, as you'll see throughout this guide, is to find the right kind of advice from the right person at the right time.

———————

Amy Gallo is a contributing editor at *Harvard Business Review*. Follow her on Twitter at @amyegallo.

Section 2
Mapping Out Your Development

Chapter 3
Reaching Your Potential

by Robert S. Kaplan

Ambitious professionals often spend a substantial amount of time thinking about strategies that will help them achieve greater levels of success. They strive for a more impressive job title, higher compensation, and responsibility for more sizable revenues, profits, and numbers of employees. Their definitions of success are often heavily influenced by family, friends, and colleagues.

Yet many ultimately find that, despite their efforts and accomplishments, they lack a true sense of professional satisfaction and fulfillment. During my career with Goldman Sachs, as well as over the past few years of teaching and coaching managers and MBA students at Harvard Business School, I have met a surprisingly large number

Reprinted from *Harvard Business Review*, July 2008 (product #R0807C)

of impressive executives who expressed deep frustration with their careers. They looked back and felt that they should have achieved more or even wished that they had chosen a different career altogether.

Consider a very successful research analyst at a large securities firm who came to see me because he was discouraged with his career progress. This was particularly ironic because he was well known, highly regarded (ranked number one in his industry sector), and well compensated. He told me that, after 10 years, he was tired of his job, disliked his boss, and felt he had no potential for further upward mobility. Most of all, he had always wanted to be an investment manager, but he had started out as an analyst and never really reassessed his career path. He felt trapped. He feared losing his stature and didn't want to let anyone down, but at the same time he didn't want to keep doing what he was doing.

As we talked, he wondered if he'd been so busy trying to reach specific milestones and impress other people that he'd lost sight of what he really enjoyed doing. The truth was that he loved analyzing stocks and assessing management teams, but he also wanted to have the responsibility for making the actual investment decisions and then be held accountable for the results. I encouraged him to take action and speak to a number of investment firms (including his current employer) about a career change. After doing this, he ultimately was offered and accepted a portfolio manager position in the asset management division of his current firm. He learned that his firm's leaders wanted to retain him regardless of job description and that they were quite surprised to find out he wanted to be on the investment side of the business. He has since become a superb investment manager, and although he wishes he'd stepped back and reexamined his career years earlier, he's thrilled that he made the switch while there was "still time."

If you are experiencing similar feelings of frustration or even regret about the direction of your career, this article is intended to help you examine the question, "Am I reaching my potential?" This is not the same as asking, "How do I rise to the top?" or "How can I be successful in my career?" Rather, it's about taking a very personal look at how *you* define success in your heart of hearts and then finding *your* path to get there.

To do that, you must step back and reassess your career—starting with the recognition that managing it is your responsibility. Too many people feel like victims in their careers, when in fact they have a substantial degree of control. Seizing control requires you to take a fresh look at your behavior in three main areas: knowing yourself, excelling at critical tasks, and demonstrating character and leadership.

Knowing Yourself

Taking responsibility for your career starts with an accurate assessment of your current skills and performance. Can you write down your two or three greatest strengths and your two or three most significant weaknesses? While most people can detail their strengths, they often struggle to identify key weaknesses. This exercise involves meaningful reflection and, almost always, requires soliciting the views of people who will tell you the brutal truth. Unfortunately, you often can't count on your boss to accurately assess your strengths or to be willing to confront you with what you're doing wrong. It's up to you to take control of this process by seeking coaching, asking for very specific feedback, and being receptive to input from a wide variety of people at various levels within your organization. This gathering of feedback needs to be an ongoing process because, as your career progresses, you will face new challenges and demands.

Recently I met with a division head of a large professional services firm. Though he'd been a rising star for several years, he felt he'd begun to stagnate. His direct reports and his CEO no longer seemed engaged and enthusiastic in their dealings with him, and he didn't know why. In our discussions, he was able to specifically describe his strengths, but when I asked about his weaknesses, he gave me fairly generic responses, such as "Maybe I'm too impatient" and "I need to raise my profile." When I pressed him about feedback from his boss he still struggled to identify even one specific weakness. I sent him off on an assignment: Interview at least five colleagues and subordinates.

He returned a few weeks later with several "surprises." He'd heard, for example, that while he was detail-oriented and decisive, he micromanaged, had a dictatorial style, and failed to listen. Armed with these insights, he sought coaching, started working on his flaws, and began regularly soliciting feedback from his colleagues and subordinates. A year later he reported that his effectiveness had improved as a result of these ongoing efforts, and he was once again feeling confident and optimistic about his career.

This type of initiative takes time, humility, and a willingness to confront weaknesses, fears, and blind spots that many of us would rather ignore. But I never cease to be impressed by the capacity of people to change and improve once they recognize their shortcomings as well as their strengths.

Of course, getting others to tell you where you're falling short isn't easy—particularly if they're your subordinates. It must be done in one-on-one conversations, and you need to give potential coaches time to learn that you're sincere. When your employees see you actually act on their feedback, they are likely to become more proactive in offering advice, because they know you value their input. Your subordinates and colleagues will also feel they have a stake in your success and that of your unit—which will make them more likely to enjoy working with you.

Once you have a grip on your strengths and weaknesses, your next challenge is to figure out what you truly enjoy doing. What's your dream job? How well does it match what you currently do? Many people either don't know what their passions are or are so focused on the views of their peers that they drift into the wrong career. I was recently approached by an MBA student who wanted advice on whether to go work for a hedge fund, a private equity firm, or an investment bank. When asked whether he had an interest in financial markets, he quickly said no. He wasn't even sure about the key tasks that each of those jobs would entail. When asked what he would do if he had $10 million in the bank, however, his answer was very clear: pursue a career in the music industry. He was a concert-level musician and loved the music business. Once he recognized how much he had been swayed by his fellow students' bias toward the lucrative financial services industry, he realized he needed to rethink his choices.

The conventional wisdom about the attractiveness of various careers changes constantly. Twenty-five years ago the medical and legal professions were considered financially rewarding and socially desirable. Today, a number of doctors and lawyers are frustrated in their jobs and realize that they might have based their career choices excessively on the views of their peers and popular opinion, instead of on whether they would actually love the work. Hedge funds and private equity are today's hot fields, but people who go into them without a strong enthusiasm for the actual tasks may find themselves starting from scratch a few years down the line. Loving what you do gives you the strength to weather personal setbacks, overcome adversity, face and address your weaknesses, and work the long hours typically needed to reach your full potential.

Excelling at Critical Tasks

It's very difficult to succeed if you don't excel at the tasks that are central to your chosen enterprise. That sounds painfully simple, but many executives fail to identify the three or four most important activities that lead to success in their job or business. If you're a medical researcher, the three keys are likely to be conducting cutting-edge research, getting published, and fund-raising. If you manage a large sales force, the crucial tasks might be attracting, retaining, and developing outstanding salespeople; customer segmentation; and client relationship management. If you're assessing a potential job move, you need to know what will drive success in the new position and, then, ask yourself whether you enjoy those key tasks. In your current job, identifying critical tasks helps you determine how to spend your time and develop your skills.

Promising leaders sometimes lose sight of this connection. Not long ago, a new division head at a large industrial company told me that he was struggling to grow sales and profits. He complained that he was spending too much time fighting fires and didn't have enough hours in the day. When I asked him to identify the three main drivers of success in his business, he realized that he wasn't sure. He spent the next several weeks interviewing staff and customers, and concluded that success in his business depended on developing close relationships with the purchasing managers at each of his top 25 customers, putting the right people in critical sales and manufacturing leadership positions, and staying at the cutting edge of product innovation. He also realized that his division was performing poorly in all three areas.

He proceeded to clear his calendar, force himself to delegate tasks that were less central to success, and focus on raising the bar in each of these areas. Six months later he reported that he had replaced a number of executives—including the sales manager and head of product development—and created an executive committee that met weekly to discuss critical business issues. He also reported that he'd become much more disciplined in matching his priorities (and those of his leadership team) with the keys to success for the business. Sales and profits began to improve, and he felt confident that he would resume his upward career trajectory.

Demonstrating Character and Leadership

While seemingly amorphous, character and leadership often make the difference between good performance and great performance. One measure of character is the

---

FOLLOW YOUR OWN PATH

Reaching your potential requires introspection and certain proactive behaviors—but it starts with a basic philosophy, or "rules of the road."

1. **Managing your career is 100% your responsibility, and you need to act accordingly.** Many promising professionals expect their superiors to mentor them, give them thoughtful coaching, provide them with challenging opportunities, and generally steer their development. Such a passive approach is likely to derail you at some point. While your superiors will play a role, your career is your own.

2. **Be wary of conventional wisdom.** It's almost always wrong—for you. Hopping on the bandwagon may feel good initially but often leads to

---

degree to which you put the interests of your company and colleagues ahead of your own. Excellent leaders are willing to do things for others without regard to what's in it for them. They coach and mentor. They have the mind-set of an owner and figure out what they would do if they were the ultimate decision maker. They're willing to make a recommendation that would benefit the organization's overall performance, possibly to the detriment of their own unit. They have the courage to trust that they will eventually be rewarded, even if their actions may not be in their own short-term interest.

painful regrets years later. To reach your potential, you must filter out peer pressure and popular opinion; assess your own passions, skills, and convictions; and then be courageous enough to act on them.

3. **Have faith that, although justice may not prevail at any given point in time, it should generally prevail over time.** When you do suffer an injustice, you need to be willing to step back and objectively assess your own role in these events. That mind-set will help you learn from inevitable setbacks and eventually bounce back. It will also help you stay focused on issues you can control as well as bolster your determination to act like the ultimate decision maker.

Being a leader also means being willing to speak up, even when you're expressing an unpopular view. CEOs' proposals often generate head nodding, even from people who secretly harbor serious reservations. In reality, most chief executives desperately want dissenting opinions so they can make better choices. While emerging leaders must use good judgment regarding the tone and timing of their dissent, they also need to be aware that they can hit a plateau by playing it safe when they should be asserting their heartfelt opinions.

One CEO recounted to me his regrets over a recent key hire. His top three reports had each interviewed the various job candidates and expressed no major concerns about the final choice. After the new hire was on board—and had begun to struggle—it came to light that two of the three senior managers had privately held significant reservations but concluded that the CEO's mind was made up and that speaking out was unwise. The CEO was furious. Though he recognized his own role in the mess (he vowed to more actively encourage dissent), he also lowered his opinion of the two executives who failed to express their views.

Otherwise confident executives sometimes overestimate the career risk of speaking up and meaningfully under-estimate the risk of staying silent. I encourage people to develop various approaches to help them overcome this hesitancy: For example, I've counseled emerging executives to save their money to build financial security and to avoid getting too emotionally attached to their jobs. Though it may seem that you'll never find another great job, you have to have faith that there are many attractive opportunities outside your firm.

In some cases, I advise people to become experts in some specific business area in order to build their confidence. I also encourage people to spend more time deciding what they truly believe versus trying to guess what the boss might want to hear. At work, as in competitive sports, you must play with confidence and even a little abandon. I've talked to several executives whose finest moments came when they gathered their courage and confidently expressed disagreement with their boss and peers. To their surprise, they found that they were treated with more respect after these episodes.

Most outstanding CEOs value emerging executives who assert themselves out of genuine concern for what is best for the company. Doing the right thing is a reward in itself—psychologically in the short run and professionally in the longer run. Of course, this approach requires that you have some reasonable level of faith that justice will prevail. I have seldom seen people hurt their careers by speaking up and appropriately articulating a well-thought-out contrary position (even when it was unpopular). However, I have seen many bitter and confused people who stalled their careers by playing it safe.

Every rewarding career will bring ups and downs, bad days, bad weeks, and bad months. Everyone will face setbacks and discouraging situations. Some people abandon their plans when they hit one of these bumps. They lose their way and ultimately undermine their own performance—and the wound is all the more painful because it is self-inflicted. The advice in this article is intended to help you avoid such self-inflicted wounds. There's nothing anyone can do to prevent you from reaching your potential; the challenge is for you to identify your dream, develop the skills to get there, and exhibit character and leadership. Then, you need to have the courage to periodically reassess, make adjustments, and pursue a course that reflects who you truly are.

Robert S. Kaplan is the acting president and CEO of Harvard Management Company and a professor of management practice at Harvard Business School in Boston. He is also a former vice chairman of the Goldman Sachs Group.

Chapter 4
Making Yourself Indispensable

by John H. Zenger, Joseph R. Folkman, and Scott K. Edinger

A manager we'll call Tom was a midlevel sales executive at a *Fortune* 500 company. After a dozen or so years there, he was thriving—he made his numbers, he was well liked, he got consistently positive reviews. He applied for a promotion that would put him in charge of a high-profile worldwide product-alignment initiative, confident that he was the top candidate and that this was the logical next move for him, a seemingly perfect fit for his skills and ambitions. His track record was solid. He'd made no stupid mistakes or career-limiting moves, and he'd had no run-ins with upper management. He was

Reprinted from *Harvard Business Review*, October 2011 (product #R1110E)

stunned, then, when a colleague with less experience got the job. What was the matter?

As far as Tom could tell, nothing. Everyone was happy with his work, his manager assured him, and a recent 360-degree assessment confirmed her view. Tom was at or above the norm in every area, strong not only in delivering results but also in problem solving, strategic thinking, and inspiring others to top performance. "No need to reinvent yourself," she said. "Just keep doing what you're doing. Go with your strengths."

But how? Tom was at a loss. Should he think more strategically? Become even more inspiring? Practice problem solving more intently?

It's pretty easy and straightforward to improve on a weakness; you can get steady, measurable results through linear development—that is, by learning and practicing basic techniques. But the data from our decades of work with tens of thousands of executives all over the world has shown us that developing strengths is very different. Doing more of what you already do well yields only incremental improvement. To get appreciably better at it, you have to work on complementary skills—what we call *nonlinear* development. This has long been familiar to athletes as cross-training. A novice runner, for example, benefits from doing stretching exercises and running a few times a week, gradually increasing mileage to build up endurance and muscle memory. But an experienced marathoner won't get significantly faster merely by running ever longer distances. To reach the next level, he needs to supplement that regimen by building up complementary skills through weight training, swimming, bicycling, interval training, yoga, and the like.

So it is with leadership competencies. To move from good to much better, you need to engage in the business equivalent of cross-training. If you're technically adept, for instance, delving even more deeply into technical manuals won't get you nearly as far as honing a complementary skill such as communication, which will make your expertise more apparent and accessible to your coworkers.

In this article we provide a simple guide to becoming a far more effective leader. We will see how Tom identified his strengths, decided which one to focus on and which complementary skill to develop, and what the results were. The process is straightforward, but complements are not always obvious. So first we'll take a closer look at the leadership equivalent of cross-training.

The Interaction Effect

In cross-training, the combination of two activities produces an improvement—an *interaction effect*—substantially greater than either one can produce on its own. There's nothing mysterious here. Combining diet with exercise, for example, has long been known to be substantially more effective in losing weight than either diet or exercise alone.

In our previous research we found 16 differentiating leadership competencies that correlate strongly with positive business outcomes such as increased profitability, employee engagement, revenue, and customer satisfaction. Among those 16, we wondered, could we find pairs that would produce significant interaction effects?

We searched through our database of more than a quarter million 360-degree surveys of some 30,000 developing leaders for pairings that resulted in far higher scores on overall leadership effectiveness than either attribute did on its own. The results were unambiguous. Take, for example, the competencies "focuses on results" and "builds relationships." Only 14% of leaders who were reasonably strong (that is, scored in the 75th percentile) in focusing on results but less so in building relationships reached the extraordinary leadership level: the 90th percentile in overall leadership effectiveness. Similarly, only 12% of those who were reasonably strong in building relationships but less so in focusing on results reached that level. But when an individual performed well in both categories, something dramatic happened: Fully 72% of those in the 75th percentile in both categories reached the 90th percentile in overall leadership effectiveness.

We measured the degree of correlation between overall leadership effectiveness and all possible pairings of our 16 differentiating competencies to learn which pairings were the most powerful. We also matched our 16 competencies with other leadership skills and measured how those pairs correlated with overall leadership effectiveness. We discovered that each of the 16 has up to a dozen associated behaviors—which we call *competency companions*—that were highly correlated with leadership excellence when combined with the differentiating competency. (For a complete list of the competencies and their companions, see the sidebar "What Skills Will Magnify My Strengths?")

Consider the main competency "displays honesty and integrity." How would a leader go about improving a relative strength in this area? By being more honest? (We've heard that answer to the question many times.) That's not particularly useful advice. If an executive were weak in this area, we could recommend various ways to improve: Behave more consistently, avoid saying one thing and doing another, follow through on stated commitments, and so on. But a leader with high integrity is most likely already doing those things.

Our competency-companion research suggests a practical path forward. For example, assertiveness is among the behaviors that when paired with honesty and integrity correlate most strongly with high levels of overall leadership effectiveness. We don't mean to imply a causal relationship here: Assertiveness doesn't make someone honest, and integrity doesn't produce assertiveness. But if a highly principled leader learned to become more assertive, he might be more likely to speak up and act with the courage of his convictions, thus applying his strength more widely or frequently to become a more effective leader.

Our data suggest other ways in which a competency companion can reinforce a leadership strength. It might make the strength more apparent, as in the case of the technically strong leader who improves her ability to communicate. Or skills learned in developing the competency companion might be profitably applied to the main competency. A leader strong in innovativeness, for instance, might learn how to champion change, thus encouraging his team to achieve results in new and more creative ways.

AN INFORMAL 360

Before you can build on your strengths, you need an objective view of what they are. Ideally, this comes from a formal, confidential 360-degree evaluation. But if that's not possible, a direct approach can work. Try simply asking your team members, colleagues, and boss these simple questions, either in person or in writing.

- What leadership skills do you think are strengths for me?

- Is there anything I do that might be considered a fatal flaw—that could derail my career or lead me to fail in my current job if it's not addressed?

- What leadership ability, if outstanding, would have the most significant impact on the productivity or effectiveness of the organization?

- What leadership abilities of mine have the most significant impact on you?

Do your best to exhibit receptiveness and to create a feeling of safety (especially for direct reports). Make it clear that you're seeking self-improvement. Tell your colleagues explicitly that you are open to negative feedback and that you will absorb it professionally and appropriately—and without retribution. Of course, you need to follow through on this promise, or the entire process will fail.

Building Strengths, Step by Step

As a practical matter, cross-training for leadership skills is clear-cut: (1) Identify your strengths. (2) Choose a strength to focus on according to its importance to the organization and how passionately you feel about it. (3) Select a complementary behavior you'd like to enhance. (4) Develop it in a linear way.

Identify your strengths

Strengths can arguably be identified in a variety of ways. But we contend that in the context of effective leadership, your view of your own (or even some perfectly objective view, supposing one could be had) is less important than other people's, because leadership is all about your effect on others. That's why we start with a 360—as Tom did.

Ideally, you should go about this in a psychometrically valid way, through a formal process in which you and your direct reports, peers, and bosses anonymously complete questionnaires ranking your leadership attributes on a quantitative scale. You and they should also answer some qualitative, open-ended questions concerning your strengths, your fatal flaws (if any), and the relative importance of those attributes to the company. By "fatal flaws," we mean flaws so critical that they can overpower any strengths you have or may develop—flaws that can derail your career.

Not every organization is able or willing to conduct 360s for everyone. So if that's not feasible, you may be able to solicit qualitative data from your colleagues if—and this is a big caveat—you can make them feel comfortable enough to be honest in their feedback. You could create your own feedback form and ask people to return it anonymously. (See the sidebar "An Informal 360" for a suggested set of questions.) We have also seen earnest one-on-one conversations work for this purpose; if nothing else, they show your coworkers that you are genuinely interested in self-improvement. (Nevertheless, it's unlikely that anyone will tell you directly if you have fatal flaws.)

In interpreting the results, people commonly focus first on their lowest scores. But unless those are extremely low (in the 10th percentile), that's a mistake. (We have found that 20% of executives do typically discover such a critical problem in their 360s; if you're among them, you must fix the flaw, which you can do in a linear way.)

What makes leaders indispensable to their organizations, our data unmistakably show, is not being good at many things but being uniquely outstanding at a few things. Such strengths allow a leader's inevitable weaknesses to be overlooked. The executives in our database who exhibited no profound (that is, in the 90th percentile) strengths scored only in the 34th percentile, on average, in overall leadership effectiveness. But if they had just one outstanding strength, their overall leadership effectiveness score rose to the 64th percentile, on average. In other words, the difference between being in the bottom third of leaders and being almost in the top third is a single extraordinary strength. Two profound strengths put leaders close to the top quartile, three put them in the top quintile, and four put them nearly in the top decile.

FIGURE 4–1

What difference can a single strength make?

Raising just one competency to the level of outstanding can up your overall
leadership effectiveness ranking from the bottom third to almost the top third.

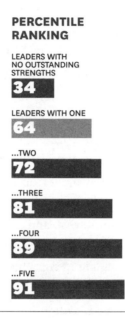

PERCENTILE RANKING

LEADERS WITH
NO OUTSTANDING
STRENGTHS
34

LEADERS WITH ONE
64

...TWO
72

...THREE
81

...FOUR
89

...FIVE
91

(See the figure "What difference can a single strength make?")

In this context, a look at Tom's 360 results sheds light on the question of why he was passed over for a plum assignment. Tom had no critical flaws, but he hadn't yet demonstrated any outstanding strengths either. With no strengths above the 70th percentile, he didn't score "good," let alone "outstanding," in overall leadership ability. Anyone in the organization with a single notable strength was likely to outpace him for promotion opportunities. But if Tom could lift just a few of his relative strengths from the 70th to the 80th and then the 90th percentile, his overall leadership effectiveness might go from above average to good to exceptional. Clearly, those strengths merited a closer examination.

Like many people, though, Tom was initially galvanized by the low bars on his chart, which evoked a mixture of guilt and denial. His relatively low score on building relationships called up uncomfortable memories of high school—something he didn't mention as he looked over the results with his boss. But he did say that he couldn't believe he wasn't scored higher on innovativeness, and he started to tick off initiatives he felt he deserved credit for. Maybe he was innovative, and maybe he wasn't. It's common for your self-assessment to vary sharply from everyone else's assessment of you. But remember that it's others' opinions that matter.

When Tom did turn his attention to his strengths, he wasn't surprised to see that he scored well in focusing on results and in solving problems and analyzing issues. Less obvious to him, and perhaps more gratifying, were his relatively high marks in developing strategic perspective and inspiring and motivating others. Now he could move on to the next step.

Choose a strength to focus on

Choices between good and bad are easy. But choices between good and good cause us to deliberate and second-guess. It may not matter which competency Tom selected, since enhancing any one of them would

WHAT SKILLS WILL MAGNIFY MY STRENGTHS?

Our research shows that 16 leadership competencies correlate strongly with positive business outcomes. Each of them has up to a dozen "competency companions" whose development will strengthen the core skill.

Character

Displays honesty and integrity

- Shows concern and consideration for others

- Is trustworthy

- Demonstrates optimism

- Is assertive

- Inspires and motivates others

- Deals well with ambiguity

- Is decisive

- Focuses on results

Personal Capability

Exhibits technical/professional expertise

- Solves problems and analyzes issues

- Builds relationships and networks

- Communicates powerfully and broadly

- Pursues excellence

(continued)

(*continued*)

- Takes initiative

- Develops others

- Displays honesty and integrity

- Acts in the team's best interest

Solves problems and analyzes issues

- Takes initiative

- Is organized and good at planning

- Is decisive

- Innovates

- Wants to tackle challenges

- Develops strategic perspective

- Acts independently

- Has technical expertise

- Communicates powerfully and broadly

Innovates

- Is willing to take risks and challenge the status quo

- Supports others in risk taking

- Solves problems and analyzes issues

- Champions change

- Learns quickly from success and failure

- Develops strategic perspective

- Takes initiative

Practices self-development

- Listens

- Is open to others' ideas

- Respects others

- Displays honesty and integrity

- Inspires and motivates others

- Provides effective feedback and development

- Takes initiative

- Is willing to take risks and challenge the status quo

Getting Results

Focuses on results

- Is organized and good at planning

- Displays honesty and integrity

- Anticipates problems

- Sees desired results clearly

(*continued*)

(*continued*)

- Provides effective feedback and development

- Establishes stretch goals

- Is personally accountable

- Is quick to act

- Provides rewards and recognition

- Creates a high-performance team

- Marshals adequate resources

- Innovates

Establishes stretch goals

- Inspires and motivates others

- Is willing to take risks and challenge the status quo

- Gains the support of others

- Develops strategic perspective

- Champions change

- Is decisive

- Has technical and business expertise

- Focuses on results

Takes initiative

- Anticipates problems

- Emphasizes speed

- Is organized and good at planning

- Champions others

- Deals well with ambiguity

- Follows through

- Inspires and motivates others

- Establishes stretch goals

- Displays honesty and integrity

Interpersonal Skills

Communicates powerfully and broadly

- Inspires and motivates others

- Develops strategic perspective

- Establishes stretch goals

- Deals effectively with the outside world

- Is trustworthy

- Involves others

- Translates messages for clarity

(continued)

(*continued*)

- Solves problems and analyzes issues

- Takes initiative

- Innovates

- Develops others

Inspires and motivates others

- Connects emotionally with others

- Establishes stretch goals

- Exhibits clear vision and direction

- Communicates powerfully and broadly

- Develops others

- Collaborates and fosters teamwork

- Nurtures innovation

- Takes initiative

- Champions change

- Is a strong role model

Builds relationships

- Collaborates and fosters teamwork

- Displays honesty and integrity

- Develops others

- Listens

- Communicates powerfully and broadly

- Provides rewards and recognition

- Practices inclusion and values diversity

- Demonstrates optimism

- Practices self-development

Develops others

- Practices self-development

- Shows concern and consideration for others

- Is motivated by the success of others

- Practices inclusion and values diversity

- Develops strategic perspective

- Provides effective feedback and development

- Inspires and motivates others

- Innovates

- Provides rewards and recognition

- Displays honesty and integrity

Collaborates and fosters teamwork

- Is trustworthy

- Builds relationships and networks

(continued)

(*continued*)

- Practices inclusion and values diversity

- Develops strategic perspective

- Establishes stretch goals

- Communicates powerfully and broadly

- Displays honesty and integrity

- Adapts to change

- Inspires and motivates others

- Develops others

Leading Change

Develops strategic perspective

- Focuses on customers

- Innovates

- Solves problems and analyzes issues

- Communicates powerfully and broadly

- Establishes stretch goals

- Demonstrates business acumen

- Champions change

- Inspires and motivates others

Champions change

- Inspires and motivates others
- Builds relationships and networks
- Develops others
- Provides rewards and recognition
- Practices inclusion and values diversity
- Innovates
- Focuses on results
- Is willing to take risks and challenge the status quo
- Develops strategic perspective

Connects the group to the outside world

- Develops broad perspective
- Develops strategic perspective
- Inspires and motivates others
- Has strong interpersonal skills
- Takes initiative
- Gathers and assimilates information
- Champions change
- Communicates powerfully and broadly

markedly improve his leadership effectiveness. Nevertheless, we recommend that developing leaders focus on a competency that matters to the organization and about which they feel some passion, because a strength you feel passionate about that is not important to your organization is essentially a hobby, and a strength the organization needs that you don't feel passionate about is just a chore.

You can use your colleagues' importance ratings from the 360 assessment to get a somewhat objective view of organizational needs. But the prospect of following his passions alarmed Tom, who didn't know how to begin. Answering a series of questions made the notion more concrete. For each of the 16 competencies, he ran down the following list:

- Do I look for ways to enhance this skill?

- Do I look for new ways to use it?

- Am I energized, not exhausted, when I use it?

- Do I pursue projects in which I can apply this strength?

- Can I imagine devoting time to improving it?

- Would I enjoy getting better at this skill?

Counting his "yes" answers gave Tom a solid way to quantify his passions. A simple worksheet showed him how his skills, his passions, and the organization's needs dovetailed (see the sidebar "Narrowing Down the Options"). When Tom checked off his top five competencies, his five passions, and the organization's top priorities, he could see a clear convergence. He decided to focus on the strength that, as it happens, we have found to be most universally associated with extraordinary leadership: "inspires and motivates others."

Select a complementary behavior

People who excel at motivating others are good at persuading them to take action and to go the extra mile. They effectively exercise power to influence key decisions for the benefit of the organization. They know how to motivate different people in different ways. So it was not surprising that Tom already did those things pretty well. He scanned the list of competency companions:

- Connects emotionally with others

- Establishes stretch goals

- Exhibits clear vision and direction

- Communicates powerfully and broadly

- Develops others

- Collaborates and fosters teamwork

- Nurtures innovation

- Takes initiative

- Champions change

- Is a strong role model

NARROWING DOWN THE OPTIONS

The strength you focus on should be both important to the organization and important to you. A simple worksheet (like Tom's, below) can help you see where your strengths and interests and the needs of your organization converge. Choose five competencies in each of the three categories.

	YOUR COMPETENCIES	YOUR PASSIONS	ORGANIZATIONAL NEEDS	TOTAL
1. DISPLAYS HONESTY AND INTEGRITY				
2. EXHIBITS TECHNICAL/PROFESSIONAL EXPERTISE	X			1
3. SOLVES PROBLEMS AND ANALYZES ISSUES	X			1
4. INNOVATES		X	X	2
5. PRACTICES SELF-DEVELOPMENT				
6. FOCUSES ON RESULTS	X			1
7. ESTABLISHES STRETCH GOALS				
8. TAKES INITIATIVE		X		1
9. COMMUNICATES POWERFULLY AND BROADLY			X	1
10. INSPIRES AND MOTIVATES OTHERS	X	X	X	③
11. BUILDS RELATIONSHIPS			X	1
12. DEVELOPS OTHERS		X		1
13. COLLABORATES AND FOSTERS TEAMWORK		X		1
14. DEVELOPS STRATEGIC PERSPECTIVE	X		X	2
15. CHAMPIONS CHANGE				
16. CONNECTS THE GROUP TO THE OUTSIDE WORLD				

You should choose a companion behavior that, like a good strength, is important to the organization and makes you feel enthusiastic about tackling it. But at this point it's also constructive to consider your lower scores. In talking these points over with his manager, Tom decided to work on his communication skills, which didn't score particularly high but were high enough that raising them a little could make a significant difference.

Develop it in a linear way

Having settled on a competency companion, Tom could now work at directly improving his basic skills in that area. Strong communicators speak concisely and deliver effective presentations. Their instructions are clear. They write well. They can explain new concepts clearly. They help people understand how their work contributes to broader business objectives. They can translate terms used by people in different functions. Tom saw lots of room for improvement here: No one would ever call him concise; he didn't always finish sentences he'd started; and he found writing a challenge.

We would have recommended that he look for as many opportunities as possible, both inside and outside work, to improve his communication. He could take a course in business writing. He could practice with friends and family, in his church or his community. He could volunteer to make presentations to senior management or ask colleagues to critique some of his memos and e-mails. He might volunteer to help high school students write college application essays. He could videotape himself making speeches or join a local Toastmasters club.

Tom decided to seek the advice of a colleague whose communication skills he admired. The colleague suggested (among other things) that because writing was not a strong point, Tom should practice communicating more in person or over the phone. This turned out to be challenging: Tom found that before he could even begin, he had to change his approach to e-mail, because he was in the habit of constantly checking and replying to it throughout the day. He couldn't always substitute the phone, because he couldn't make calls while he was in a meeting or talking to someone else. He started to set aside specific times of the day for e-mail so that he could reply by phone or in person—a small change that had unexpected consequences. Instead of being interrupted and distracted at random moments throughout the day (and evening), his staffers had concentrated, direct interactions with him. They found these more efficient and effective, even though they could no longer choose when (or whether) to reply to Tom's cryptic e-mails. Tom found that he connected better with people he talked to, both because his attention wasn't divided between them and his BlackBerry and because he could read their tone of voice and body language. As a result, he absorbed more information, and his colleagues felt he was more attentive to their views.

Tom also started to pay more attention not just to how he was communicating but to what he was saying. His colleague suggested that Tom start to keep track of how often he issued instructions versus how often he asked questions. Tom also took note of how much of what he said was criticism (constructive or otherwise) and how much was encouragement. Increasing the proportion of questions and encouragement had an immediate effect: His team began to understand him more quickly, so he didn't have to repeat himself as often. Several team members actually thanked him for allowing them to express their points of view.

Like Tom, you should expect to see some concrete evidence of improvement within 30 to 60 days. If you don't, what you're doing is not working. That said, complementary behaviors improve steadily with practice, and Tom's progress is typical: Fifteen months later, on taking another 360, he found he'd moved into the 82nd percentile in his ability to inspire. He wasn't extraordinary yet, but he was getting close. Our advice would be to keep at it—to improve another competency companion or two until he reaches the 90th percentile and becomes truly exceptional at inspiring others. Then he can start the entire process again with another strength and its complements, and another—at which point he will be making a uniquely valuable contribution to his company.

Can You Overdo It?

Everyone knows someone who is too assertive, too technically oriented, too focused on driving for results. Many people cite examples like these to argue against the wisdom of improving your leadership effectiveness by strengthening your strengths. Our research does in fact show a point where balance becomes important. The data suggest that the difference between having four profound strengths and having five is a gain of merely 2 percentage points in overall leadership effectiveness. Thus leaders who are already exceptional should consider one more variable.

You will note in the sidebar "What Skills Will Magnify My Strengths?" that the 10 differentiating competencies fall into five broader categories: character, personal capability, getting results, interpersonal skills, and leading change. People who have many strengths should consider how they are distributed across those categories and focus improvement efforts on an underrepresented one.

But we cannot think of a less constructive approach to improving your leadership effectiveness than treating your strengths as weaknesses. Have you ever known anyone who had too much integrity? Was too effective a communicator? Was just too inspiring? Developing competency companions works precisely because, rather than simply doing more of the same, you are enhancing how you already behave with new ways of working and interacting that will make that behavior more effective.

Focusing on your strengths is hardly a new idea. Forty-four years ago Peter Drucker made the business case eloquently in *The Effective Executive:* "Unless . . . an executive looks for strength and works at making strength productive, he will only get the impact of what a man cannot do, of his lacks, his weaknesses, his impediments to performance and effectiveness. To staff from what there is not and to focus on weakness is wasteful—a misuse, if not abuse, of the human resource." Since then a body of work has grown up supporting and advocating for Drucker's approach. Our own research shows how big a difference developing a few strengths can make. It is distressing to find that fewer than 10% of the executives we work with have any plan to do so.

We are convinced that the problem is less a matter of conviction than of execution. Executives need a path to enhancing their strengths that is as clear as the one to fixing their weaknesses. That is the greatest value, we believe, of the cross-training approach: It allows people to use the linear improvement techniques they know and understand to produce a nonlinear result.

Often executives complain to us that there are not enough good leaders in their organizations. We would argue that in fact far too many leaders are merely good. The challenge is not to replace bad leaders with good ones; it is to turn people like Tom—hardworking, capable executives who are reasonably good at their jobs—into outstanding leaders with distinctive strengths

---

John H. Zenger is the CEO, **Joseph R. Folkman** is the president, and **Scott K. Edinger** is the executive vice president of Zenger Folkman, a leadership development consultancy. They are the authors of *The Inspiring Leader* (McGraw-Hill, 2009).

Chapter 5
Why You Didn't Get That Promotion

by John Beeson

You've been passed over for a key promotion despite stellar results and glowing reviews. You've asked where you're falling short, but the responses have been vague and unsatisfying, leaving you angry, frustrated, and unsure of how to get ahead. Promotion decisions seem arbitrary and political. What's going on?

In most organizations, promotions are governed by unwritten rules—the often fuzzy, intuitive, and poorly expressed feelings of senior executives regarding individuals' ability to succeed in C-suite positions. As an aspiring executive, you might not know those rules, much less the specific skills you need to develop or demonstrate

Reprinted from *Harvard Business Review*, June 2009 (product #R0906L)

to follow them. The bottom line: You're left to your own devices in interpreting feedback and finding a way to achieve your career goals.

That's what happened to Ralph Thomas, the vice president of operations for Smith & Mullins's industrial products division, the company's largest operating group. (All names and identifying details in this article are disguised.) He wasn't blindsided by the announcement that Kelly Ferguson had been promoted to senior vice president and general manager for corporate markets—he'd been informed the week before. But Ralph had been a contender, and this was the second time in four years he'd missed out on a division GM job. The first time, Smith & Mullins had hired an outsider who later left the position for a major role at a rival firm.

Ralph always had excellent performance reviews. His 360 results indicated that people loved working for him, and as far as he could tell, managers across the company were beating down the doors to join his group. In terms of execution, his track record was flawless: He and his team had met or surpassed their numbers in each of the past five years. Additionally, they had successfully implemented every major corporate program during that time, and his division had recently been selected to serve as the pilot site for an SAP installation. When he'd learned of these last two GM assignments, he'd also been told that he had a great future with the company and that with a little "seasoning," he'd be ready for advancement. He'd tried several times to get the real scoop on why he hadn't been promoted, only to hear vague comments about improving his "communication skills" and demonstrating more "executive presence" and "leadership." It seemed to him that the company valued people who could look and sound good in the boardroom more than it cared about the year-over-year results of proven performers like himself.

As for Kelly? She'd hired some top people in the past couple of years, but Ralph knew that she had a reputation for being tough on her reports and having "sharp elbows." To Ralph, the promotion wasn't much of an expression of the company's leadership competency model, posted on his office wall: "Display ethics and integrity, envision the future, deliver results, focus on customers, engage in teamwork and collaboration, and develop talent." Ralph bore Kelly no ill will, but it looked as though it was time to update his résumé and rekindle some relationships in his network. Distasteful as it was, testing the job market seemed to be the only way to advance.

The Unwritten Rules

Ralph's situation is surprisingly common, especially among people who aren't politically inclined. Few organizations spell out the criteria for advancement.

Though Ralph had been considered for the GM role both times, in each instance there were bona fide concerns about his readiness. The vague feedback about his communication skills actually alluded to tensions with peers in other units: He could be overly competitive and slow to resolve conflict, whereas Kelly's powers of persuasion allowed her to manage discord and achieve superior results. She was also known for developing talent. Working for her was not for the faint of heart, but she challenged her staff members, and they grew in the process. Ralph didn't recognize that his popularity reflected, in part, his reputation for being a little easy on people— he didn't stretch them to grow and develop. Managers flocking to his unit were often B players who knew he'd cut them some slack. He was luring talent that was good but not great; Kelly was attracting A players who wanted a push. The company's competency model included "develop talent" but didn't specify that having a track record for doing so was nonnegotiable for anyone who wanted to rise beyond Ralph's level.

Under the heading of "leadership" lurked questions regarding Ralph's strategic thinking. He was a go-to guy for implementing corporate initiatives, a master of continuous improvement. But senior management had seen no evidence of his ability to conceive a large-scale change that would produce a quantum leap in performance. Can strategic thinking be developed? That's open to debate, but the fact was that Ralph had always worked for visionaries who never gave him the chance to flex his own strategic muscles, a problem everyone had overlooked.

The information void wasn't a matter of malice; rather, it was due to assumptions that nobody thought to make explicit and an all-too-human reluctance to deliver bad news. Managers and HR professionals often provide intentionally vague feedback for fear of losing a good employee. Further, although most leadership competency models refer in some way to important management skills and attributes, they typically fail to distinguish nice-to-have from nonnegotiable skills.

What's more, such models usually don't spell out how leadership skills should be demonstrated at different levels or how the relative importance of those qualities will change as you rise in the hierarchy. For example, in middle management, teamwork—defined as the ability to maintain cohesion and morale within one's group—is a vital competency. At higher levels, where Ralph hopes to play, it matters less. In fact, at most companies, cohesion tends to fall short at senior levels thanks to rivalry and ego, but teams function pretty well nonetheless. Acquiring and developing talent is the executive's imperative, and teamwork becomes a nice-to-have. Ralph's ability to orchestrate well-functioning teams to complete complex projects, among other skills, had singled him out for previous promotions. But when he was being considered for the GM jobs, strategic thinking became a much higher priority.

Many of the unwritten rules are especially hard to nail down because they don't pertain to technical ability, industry experience, or business knowledge. Rather, they relate to the "soft" skills that combine to give decision makers an intuitive sense of whether a candidate will succeed at the senior level. And, as predictable career paths become more or less extinct, the confusion for people seeking advancement just gets worse.

In my 30 years of experience in and observation of succession planning and executive development at large companies, I've found that the unwritten rules of C-suite placement decisions fall into three categories. *Nonnegotiables* are the fundamental factors without which an executive will not be considered for promotion. *Deselection factors* are characteristics that eliminate an otherwise qualified candidate from consideration. *Core selection factors* are what ultimately dictate promotion decisions. The sidebar "Key Factors in Executive Career Advancement" shows the model I've developed for senior managers. The factors may differ at your company, but the ones highlighted in the sidebar are pretty typical.

Ralph passes the test on the nonnegotiables and the deselection factors but falls short on several core selection factors, like thinking strategically, building a strong executive team, and having the organization savvy to work effectively across internal boundaries. If Smith & Mullins made a list of such factors available to its executives, along with a dose of constructive feedback, Ralph would probably be able to see where he needs to devote his energies.

But since it doesn't, Ralph has to tease out the underlying issues. Although he periodically gets feedback from 360s, such reviews—unless combined with confidential face-to-face interviews by a third party—are rarely sufficient to illuminate the core reasons behind a stalled career.

One obvious way to get insight is to approach your boss and colleagues directly for their opinions, though their input might be of limited use. They may not be straight with you, and their perspectives may differ from those of the most senior decision makers. For additional information, you might have a conversation with your former manager or your boss's boss. Try to contact the highest-level manager who is knowledgeable about your work and with whom you have a positive relationship, so your approach seems natural and appropriate. (Caveat: Don't go behind your boss's back. He or she should know about any contact with other executives and what your intentions are.) For the reasons stated earlier, you'll probably have to dig a little to get useful information. That's not easy, so let's take a closer look at how you can go about having a truly constructive conversation.

How to Ask, How to Listen

Getting past executives' reluctance to provide direct and difficult feedback is tricky. When asking for input, project a sincere desire to understand what's holding you back—and avoid appearing to lobby or argue. Your core question should be "What skills and capabilities do I need to demonstrate in order to be a strong candidate for higher levels of responsibility at some point in the future?"

Get into active-listening mode. Any comment or body language that conveys defensiveness will most likely cause the other person to either clam up or move the conversation to easier (and vaguer) territory—such as the need for more "seasoning" that Ralph kept hearing about. Ask clarifying questions, but don't challenge the content. (You can attempt to correct factual errors with the right person later; this isn't the time.) Be alert to code words and phrases masking fundamental issues—general observations about the need for "increased leadership ability" or "better teamwork" or "improved communication."

For instance, a manager I'll call Terry was told by her boss that she needed to improve her leadership skills before she'd be eligible for her next promotion. She was

KEY FACTORS IN EXECUTIVE CAREER ADVANCEMENT

Nonnegotiables

Factors that are absolutely necessary for you to be a contender

- Demonstrating consistently strong performance

- Displaying ethics, integrity, and character

- Being driven to lead and to assume higher levels of responsibility

Deselection Factors

Characteristics that prevent you from being considered as a serious candidate

- Having weak interpersonal skills

- Treating others with insensitivity or abrasiveness

- Putting self-interest above company good

- Holding a narrow, parochial perspective on the business and the organization

Core Selection Factors

Capabilities that breed others' confidence in your ability to succeed at the senior executive level

- Setting direction and thinking strategically; spotting marketplace trends and developing a winning strategy that differentiates the company

- Building and continually upgrading a strong executive team; having a "nose for talent"; establishing an adequate level of team cohesion

- Managing implementation without getting involved at too low a level of detail; defining a set of roles, processes, and measures to ensure that things get done reliably

- Building the capacity for innovation and change; knowing when new ways of doing business are required; having the courage, tolerance for risk, and change-management skills to bring new ideas to fruition

- Getting things done across internal boundaries (lateral management); demonstrating organization savvy; influencing and persuading colleagues; dealing well with conflict

- Growing and developing as an executive; soliciting and responding to feedback; adjusting leadership style in light of experience

managing multiple initiatives, and her teams were functioning effectively; she didn't see how to improve her leadership except by taking on more projects. Fortunately, she had worked for her boss's manager earlier in her career and could set up a meeting. In a series of probing questions, she asked the manager to help her define what "better leadership" would be in her case. She discovered that in her dedication she in fact had been doing herself a disservice. She'd been given an ever-increasing number of projects because of her superior organizational and people-management skills and her ability to stay on top of details. However, senior managers were concerned that she was maxed out by her personal involvement in every initiative and wanted to see that she could delegate more and create processes and systems that would ensure flawless execution without so much direct supervision.

In response she put considerable effort into rethinking how she spent her time: which issues she should be involved in personally, which she could—with some coaching—learn to delegate to others, and what kinds of meetings and reports would allow her to stay as close to projects as was needed. She revamped her team's staff meeting and the level of preparation required. She also designated a direct report as chief of staff to follow up on deadlines and alert her to situations that required her intervention. Terry admits that it was initially difficult to extricate herself from the details on some projects and confesses to poring over the status reports submitted by the staff. But with practice she got better at letting go. A year later she was promoted to lead a large operational unit.

Things don't always work out so well. Ed, a highly proficient finance manager, had advanced quickly because of his technical knowledge but recently missed out on several key promotions. His boss told him not to worry, everything was fine. Still, Ed met with his unit's HR manager, who advised him to improve his communication skills. This confused him; he took pride in his ability to write and speak clearly and devoted a lot of time to communicating with his staff. At the suggestion of the HR manager, he met with three peers to get their opinions. All three were hesitant to offer their opinions until Ed probed specifically for examples of poor communication on his part. It turned out that he was right; his basic communication skills were fine. Rather, the underlying issue lay with his ability to listen and to be flexible. Colleagues complained that he tended to get locked into his own opinions, that he lacked openness to other perspectives and shut down creative alternatives. Some considered him arrogant.

Overall, his peers recommended that Ed spend more time discussing his plans with them and soliciting input. Unfortunately, Ed saw this as "politics" and energy that would be diverted from getting things done. Exacerbating the situation was the fact that Ed's boss was encouraging him to drive the implementation of a new corporate policy that Ed's peers found onerous. When his boss took a new position within the company, Ed suddenly felt vulnerable. Using his extensive industry network, he quickly found another position with a well-regarded firm but ended up leaving his new job after only nine months. The official reason was that Ed was not a cultural fit in a highly collaborative environment. In reality Ed's peers at the new company complained that he was a know-it-all who tried to sell major initiatives to his boss without taking the time to understand how the organization worked and what internal customers needed.

If you are having trouble decoding the feedback you receive, try asking at the end of each session, "What one or two things—above all others—would most build confidence in my ability to succeed at higher levels within the organization?" As long as the other person answers honestly, this question tends to circumvent vagueness and separate the wheat from the chaff.

Keep in mind that changing deep-seated perceptions about you, formed over years, requires visible and consistent effort—which is why it is typically best to focus on one or two key areas of development. Think through whether your current position provides you with a platform to demonstrate needed skills. Ralph, for instance, may need to move to a position where his breakthrough thinking isn't preempted by a visionary boss. Alternatively, he may find ample opportunities to exhibit strategic thinking in his current role—if he is aggressive and creative in pursuing them and his boss gives him room to experiment.

Although this type of development isn't easy, the payoff can be huge for both the individual and the organization. Employees like Ralph learn what's really holding them back, and companies like Smith & Mullins get a deeper and better bench.

John Beeson is the principal of Beeson Consulting, which specializes in succession planning, executive development, and organization design. He is based in New York.

Section 3
Growth and Advancement

Chapter 6
Finding the Right Mentors

by Diane Coutu

If you're waiting for a wise, dedicated mentor to recognize your potential and lead you down the yellow brick road to happiness and fortune, you'll be waiting a long time—and even then you're likely to be disappointed. To exploit your opportunities to grow and move ahead in your work and your life, your best bet will always be to take matters into your own hands and seek out the people who can help you.

Before you decide which ones to turn to, though, you'll have to figure out what kinds of mentors will best meet your needs. In my own long experience on both sides of the mentoring relationship, I've come across three distinct typco:

The co-mentor: This can be anyone—a peer, a colleague, a friend—who needs you as much as you need him

A relationship between equals, co-mentoring is rooted in the desire for skill or knowledge exchange. For that reason, it's often more short-lived than a top-down mentoring relationship. It dissolves when both parties have achieved their goals. When people co-mentor each other, they typically want to learn something very specific: They may want to become proficient in a software program, for example, or better at speaking a foreign language.

My colleague David and I co-mentored each other years ago as senior editors at *Harvard Business Review*. We had a number of things in common: He was European; I had lived in Europe for 20 years. We had both studied at Oxford University and had lived in Germany. But it was what we *didn't* share that brought us into our co-mentoring relationship. He had an MBA and was a banker; I had studied literature, philosophy, and psychology and was a journalist. He understood business strategy and finance and could write case studies; I understood leadership and organizational development, and I knew how to report on those topics. We both came to our senior editor positions at HBR with significant strengths—but we also had deep holes in our knowledge and capabilities.

Together, though, we were a cohesive whole. We moved into the same office and worked at the same computer, sometimes with four hands on one keyboard, teaching each other how to develop HBR articles. We

Find a co-mentor if...

- You have a specific skill to learn.

- You have something to teach in return.

Find a remote mentor if...

- You need a fresh perspective.

- You've exhausted mentoring resources closer to you.

Find an invisible mentor if...

- You can't find a co-mentor or remote mentor to provide the right guidance or support.

- You can get what you need learning by example, with no interaction.

became increasingly productive as we learned more about editing and more about each other's skills. Our co-mentoring relationship lasted about a year and a half, and during that time we learned how to succeed on our own as generalists. Although we remained good friends and continued to offer advice on each other's articles, we'd become self-sufficient. The co-mentoring had served its purpose—ending it was the right thing to do.

Though chances are good you can't move into the same office as your co-mentor, you can set the stage for your own meaningful give-and-take in other ways. Try meeting regularly for a working breakfast or lunch, for example, or scheduling video chats on Skype—a medium that's conducive to hands-on teaching and learning because your computer and files are right there while you're using it.

The remote mentor: This is someone outside your organization who can offer a fresh perspective and objective advice

Though mentors from your company can be invaluable, given their familiarity with the culture and the key players, certain needs are best served by outside, or "remote," mentors. Suppose your unit needs to downsize, and you have to decide which people to keep on staff when there isn't any dead weight to shed. If the senior managers you work with are short on creative ideas for solving the problem because it's the first time they've faced it, you may want to consult with someone who has orchestrated a successful reorg at another company altogether. Or say you're being groomed to lead your department or unit, and everybody knows it. You've got a lot of important learning to do, but people may not be open with their feedback, even when you ask for it directly. Sometimes they bite their tongues or, worse, stroke your ego, afraid that anything they say now might count against them when you take the reins. Look for one or more mentors on the outside to get you up to speed on setting agendas, building teams, delegating, and other senior management skills.

Remote mentors can be family members, friends, old college professors—anyone in another company or another industry. They can even be strangers.

That was the case with a mentor I'll call Jon. When I was 35, on leave from the *Wall Street Journal Europe,* I decided to work on a short memoir about being a pioneering woman in the 1970s. I had never taken a creative writing course, had never published anything besides journalistic articles, and had nothing but hope—and stories—to fuel my efforts. Though I had the discipline to write every day, I knew I needed instruction in the craft of creative nonfiction: How do you tell a compelling personal story that will resonate for others? How much detail is too much? How do you avoid the narcissistic traps that so many memoir writers fall into?

Living in Brussels at a time before there was much remote learning going on in universities, I didn't have ready access to the relevant courses in English. I had also exhausted the other mentoring resources around me. So I sought out writers who shared my interest in psychology, writers whose creative work I admired. I read biographies and narrowed my search to authors whose backgrounds and sensibilities intersected with mine. After poring over their letters, essays, fiction, and whatever else they had produced, I sat down and sent out 15 customized letters asking for help. Because my search was so targeted, it was very successful—every writer responded. Two offered to work with me through correspondence. I chose Jon for his sense of humor, and so our remote mentoring relationship began.

We never met; we never spoke on the phone. But we exchanged letters almost every week. I sent him pages of prose, which he marked up in red, teaching me about voice and pacing and segues from scene to scene. Even after I finally had a decent manuscript, Jon and I continued our correspondence until he died a few years later. The relationship was remote in the truest sense: He wrote to me only after I wrote to him. The advice was never unsolicited or paternalistic, and it was always in direct response to a question I had asked. In return, he asked me to critique his published works. I offered as much constructive criticism to him as he had to me—and in doing so, I honed a skill that was essential to my work as an editor both at McKinsey & Company and *Harvard Business Review:* giving honest, sometimes tough, feedback to authors.

The invisible mentor: This is someone you learn from with little or no direct interaction

Choreographer and dancer Twyla Tharp knew that George Balanchine, the larger-than-life artistic director of the New York City Ballet, was the person she would learn from the most, structurally and musically. They met only three times—he didn't teach open classes, so she couldn't simply sign up for one—yet he served as her invisible mentor for 20 years. As Tharp explained when I interviewed her for an HBR article: "I mentally parked him in the corner of my studio, and the insistence on thoroughness that I saw in him became my standard."

A mentor like that doesn't have a personal relationship with you but can be crucial to your development. Invisible mentors may be unresponsive or deceased, or even authors of books that speak to you. "When someone asks me how to find a mentor," Tharp told me, "I tell them, 'Just go to Barnes & Noble and pull down a book from a shelf—pick out a writer, pick out a thinker. Pick out somebody who can teach you something.'" History is filled with people who turned to books for their mentoring. John F. Kennedy read Winston Churchill; Bill Clinton read Kennedy.

My literary mentor is Emily Dickinson. At every stage of my life, she's had something to offer—whether I was studying the Holy Ghost in the fourth grade or struggling to understand human psychology when I was 30. I identified with Dickinson because she was an utterly free thinker. Her belief about the role of women in society was as complex and unconventional as she was. But above all she was a brilliant writer—someone who kept reaching out for mentors, and who kept writing to them, even though they didn't help her find success (in the traditional sense) during her lifetime. When I tried my own hand at writing, she provided inspiration, wisdom, solace, and companionship.

So how can you choose your own invisible mentors? Think about the leaders, thinkers, entrepreneurs, inventors, artists, athletes, and others at the top of their game who move you. *Why* do they move you? Is it because of their craftsmanship? Their drive to excel? Their creativity? Their integrity? That "why" will shine a light on values and talents they can, by example, help you cultivate.

No matter what type of mentoring relationship you're in, it must have clear boundaries. You can deliberately draw and observe them, or the situation (a firm deadline, for instance) may *force* them. Either way, you need sharp lines to keep you out of murky personal territory: If you start expecting intimacy from your mentor, for example, or looking at him as the father you never had, you're headed for trouble and disappointment.

That said, feeling connected is key—whether it's with a co-mentor, who benefits from the relationship as much as you do; a remote mentor, who interacts with you thoughtfully but from a distance; or an invisible mentor, who has no idea you exist but calls out to you all the same. "Clicking" with someone you look up to empowers and motivates you to do your best work. Sometimes that matters even more than expertise.

———————

Diane Coutu is the director of client communications at Banyan Family Business Advisors. She also mentors high school students through the college application process.

Chapter 7
Defining Your Goals and Expectations

To set your mentoring relationship up for success, you have to decide what exactly you want to learn. "Do you want technical or strategic expertise?" asks Leslie Camino-Markowitz, director of Next Generation Leadership Development Programs at Agilent Technologies. "Cultural awareness of how business is done? Perhaps expertise in Asia?"

How do you come up with your objectives? Try using the following questions to guide your thinking.

1. What do you really want to be and do? Examine not only your business goals but also your driving passions in life.

Adapted from *Harvard Management Update*, March 2008 (product #U0803B), and from content posted on hbr.org on March 25, 2009

2. What are you doing well that will help you get there? Which core strengths will best serve you? Your ability to lead and motivate your staff? Your careful management of detailed operations?

3. What are you *not* doing well that will prevent you from getting there? Take an honest look at the roadblocks, challenges, or weaknesses that are slowing you down.

4. What will you do differently tomorrow to meet those challenges? When you practice your tennis, do you tend to favor your forehand? How will you start giving your professional "backhand" the attention it requires?

5. Where do you need the most help—and who can provide it? Now that you've worked your way through the previous questions, you're ready to articulate your goals for the mentoring relationship and map them to potential mentors who have the strengths, relationships, and resources to help you.

Stick to four or five goals for the relationship. If you include more than that, you'll have trouble taking in what your mentor has to offer. And be sure to spell them out for the person who agrees to mentor you.

Steve Trautman, author of *Teach What You Know: A Practical Leader's Guide to Knowledge Transfer Using Peer Mentoring* (Prentice-Hall, 2006), tells an all-too-familiar story about what happens when you don't:

Ross and Julie are a mentor/protégé pair who have worked together for six months with little progress. They started down this road because one day, their boss had told Ross, "Hey, you should be Julie's mentor." Both Ross and Julie are often out of the office at meetings. They never sat down to clarify [expectations], such as when and how often they would meet and who would set up those conversations. Ross and Julie's boss did not define the skills that Ross should teach Julie or even topics of conversation. Julie was worried about bothering Ross, and Ross did not want to presume Julie needed help.

If Julie had gone to her boss for more detail on which challenges he thought Ross could help her with and taken the time to assess her own goals for learning and growth, she could have roughed out a game plan with Ross. That small but crucial bit of direction would have led to a more focused and fruitful relationship.

Chapter 8
Starting and Maintaining Relationships with Mentors

by Lew McCreary

Years ago, I failed to go out and get the mentoring I needed. I was then in the midst of my first magazine launch. I had always worked on the editorial side of the company, with little exposure to sales and marketing. Nonetheless, I claimed for myself the grand dual title of editor in chief and publisher—wanting a stake in the magazine's business future, not just its content. My boss, despite some skepticism, indulged me. But soon enough, I recognized that I was in over my head and would benefit from the guidance of someone with sales acumen and objective distance from my business unit's maverick culture. I even picked out an especially good candidate: a seasoned executive from another unit who had a strong track record on the commercial side and a firm grasp of editorial values and practice.

Many times I came close to asking him to mentor me, confident he would agree to it. However, something always stopped me: I'd been given responsibilities that exceeded my experience—and, I feared, my abilities. That's not uncommon, of course. Throughout our careers, we must stretch and grow. I just wasn't sure I wanted to admit to anyone that I felt overwhelmed by the challenge. Would others start doubting me the way I secretly doubted myself? And if I did start a mentoring relationship with my executive of choice, how candid could I safely be about my colleagues, up to and including my boss?

If you're on the verge of reaching out to a mentor, you'll face difficult questions like these. The risks are real, but don't let them stymie you as they did me. Instead, keep them in check with a few ground rules for establishing and maintaining a strong, productive mentoring relationship.

Getting It Going

Here are some principles that will help you get started whether you're creating your own mentoring experiences from scratch, as many of us have to do, or participating in a formal program.

Selecting appropriate mentors

The first hurdle is picking the right people to guide you. If your company has a formal program, you may have a roster of mentors to choose from. If it doesn't, you'll need to narrow the field yourself. (See "Finding the Right Mentors" by Diane Coutu.) As you consider colleagues and people outside your unit or company, look for someone with experience that suits your goals. The executive I nearly asked for mentoring had mastered the trick I wanted to learn: transitioning into the publisher role. But a mirror image isn't always the best choice. Sometimes difference is more valuable than similarity. For example, in my more recent career, I mentored someone from the sales function. He was seeking a better understanding of the editorial operation and of the larger company culture, which I had lived in and helped shape for more than 15 years.

Ideally, you'll figure out early on whether you and your mentor are well matched. But even if it takes you awhile to conclude you're not (we often suspend disbelief about initial impressions that prove truer than we'd hoped), cut bait as soon as you figure that out. Hanging on will just be a waste of your time—and your mentor's.

Getting to know your mentor

Once you've sized up your mentoring needs and identified the right person (or people) to help you meet them, there's plenty yet to do. Kicking off a relationship may take more time and effort than you'd think. Michael Kohlman, an IT executive at a medical device manufacturer, says he and his mentor devoted their first three sessions last year to "getting an understanding of who we both were and what I wanted and needed."

Why did their preliminary work take so long? In part because they were interacting remotely, via teleconference, e-mail, and the occasional webcast. "With a long-distance relationship, you lose a number of the cues we take for granted in face-to-face communication," Kohlman says. "That doesn't mean a distance-based relationship can't work, but it does require more up-front investment."

But even if you've got proximity going for you, starting a mentoring relationship involves sharing and discovery on both sides, which may take a couple of sessions. Kohlman and his mentor—a long-tenured CIO—found they had much in common. Both had specialized in IT infrastructure and operations, and both had spent most of their careers in life-sciences companies. That gave them a lot to talk about—time well spent, in Kohlman's view.

Still, there are some shortcuts worth considering. Before you begin your mentoring sessions, you may want to complete the Myers-Briggs Type Indicator or some comparable personality assessment, if you haven't already done so. I've worked with business coaches who use such tools to help them understand their clients (and help the clients understand themselves). Why not apply them in your mentoring relationship?

The results can give you and your mentor quick insight into your strengths and preferred styles of work, collaboration, and leadership. When you meet, you can say, for instance, "I'm an INTP" (it stands for Introversion, Intuition, Thinking, and Perceiving). If it's been awhile since your mentor has visited the Myers-Briggs website (www.myersbriggs.org), remind her what INTP means: You're interested more in ideas than in social interaction, you're flexible and adaptable, you'll focus deeply on whatever problems you are called on to solve, and you're skeptical by nature.

If you have concerns about entering the relationship, air them at the start. You might want to begin with confidentiality, the big mental hurdle that kept me from enlisting a mentor. Productive mentoring demands candor— admitting your mistakes and revealing your fears, doubts, and limitations. You'll need the mentoring equivalent of the Las Vegas Rule: What happens there *stays* there. Confidentiality has to be an explicit covenant. Don't leave it to your mentor's good judgment not to let it slip to your boss that he's helping you conquer your morbid fear of delivering presentations to the executive committee.

The discretion should be mutual. Your mentor might want the freedom to disclose to you details of business life that are, strictly speaking, some distance above your pay grade. If he doesn't bring this up, raise it yourself. You'll learn more from your mentor if he knows you're not someone who talks out of school.

You can also speed up the getting-to-know-you process by bringing to one of those early sessions a list of *recent* situations that have caused you difficulty. Pick examples that speak to your mentoring objectives. For instance, if you need help in managing up, you should probably recount yesterday's contentious conversation with your boss about budgeting for expensive advanced encryption software to secure corporate information stored in the cloud. Much as your boss loves the idea of the cloud, he's less keen on the cost of making it work. Ask your mentor for advice: How can you get your boss to trust—not micromanage—the routine recommendations you make?

Such concrete examples are like case studies, only better: They'll ground your mentoring conversations in the very reality you're trying to improve. Extract from them three to five key areas where you need to develop expertise or comfort.

Creating milestones

After articulating your goals, you'll need to chart a clear path to get where you're going. Work with your mentor to create milestones—they'll give your plans direction and, just as important, help you measure your progress. Shelley Lineham, a senior IT director at a large energy retailer, finds them essential to making headway in both formal and informal mentoring environments. Without milestones, she says, "it's not so clear where you started, what you got out of the relationship, and how that benefited you at the end." Lineham actually prefers formal programs because they often *provide* basic milestones that you can then tailor to your needs. But if you're on your own, map out your mentoring in much the same way you'd manage a large project—by breaking your goals into manageable, measurable chunks.

To expedite the process, try drafting a list of milestones yourself and then asking your mentor for feedback. Say your goal is to become better at internally marketing the work of your crack SWAT team of process innovators. Identify ways to show your mastery of discrete areas of marketing competency: for example, creating metrics that capture the speed with which your team goes from concept to delivery of a newly designed process; developing outreach initiatives, such as rapid-prototyping demonstration sessions, to build demand for the team's services; publishing the internal equivalent of a marketing brochure for your team; and delivering a PowerPoint presentation of ROI case studies at an all-hands business-unit meeting. Lineham advises building in checkpoints for reflecting on what you've gained by achieving each milestone. Step back and ask yourself whether the milestones in front of you still make sense and build on what you've already accomplished.

As you're charting your path, you'll also need to agree on its length. Work with your mentor to determine a time frame for achieving your goals. The notion of an open-ended relationship may be appealing if you have a lot to learn—but you and your mentor will both find it easier to stay productive with a time commitment that's reasonably clear from the outset. You can always reassess your projected end point after you've hit a few milestones.

Sorting out logistics

One more way to set the stage for mentoring success is attending to logistics: If you hate the telephone, try to arrange in-person meetings. If your energies are at low ebb late in the day, aim for morning sessions. These details may seem small, but they affect the quality of the exchange. Defer, of course, to your mentor's preferences. She's more likely to give you time and attention if the arrangement is convenient and comfortable for her.

Keeping It Going

Now that you've established your expectations for the relationship, you're ready to make progress—and measure it. The milestones you've agreed on will keep you honest and help you get value from your mentoring over time. But you'll need more than that to maintain your momentum.

Providing structure

To keep the mentoring relationship going, you'll need structure—and it's up to you, the mentee, to supply it. Set up regular meetings with agendas so your conversations won't degenerate into aimless bull sessions, where the mentor holds forth on the triumphs of a sparkling career. Base your agendas on an overall plan—for example, "I want to develop, put forward, and win leadership approval for one entrepreneurial idea within the next year"—and make sure each meeting moves you closer to your objective.

Formal programs' processes can add structure and help you stay focused and motivated. Shelley Lineham joined a yearlong program called Pathways—an offering of the CIO Executive Council, which caters exclusively to IT professionals' career development. (Michael Kohlman is also a participant. See the sidebar "Formal Mentoring Programs" for a description of his Pathways experience.) The program's structure helped Lineham push herself to tackle one of her main goals: balancing her personal life with the growing demands of work.

Pathways provides mentees with a menu of activities and resources—including participation in webcasts, seminars, discussion boards, and professional groups. Lineham took full advantage of these suggestions. Her mentor encouraged her to join Women in Technology International (WITI), a group dedicated to helping women achieve their potential in a field long dominated by men. She attended both online and in-person events, and learned through discussions with other participants how they've managed to meet the demands of a career in IT while maintaining life balance.

Seek only enough structure to keep yourself fully engaged and making progress—and not so much as to stifle spontaneous exploration. Allow room to go in unexpected directions when circumstances warrant—for instance, when an opportunity or crisis presents itself, and your mentor can help guide you through it. Also, make time in each meeting for a "news of the week" segment, where you recount one or two anecdotes that show progress on your goals or highlight challenges that keep tripping you up.

Expecting rigor

Beware of mentoring that demands too little of you: If your mentor isn't providing regular assignments that sync up with your overall plan, ask for them, and work them into your agendas. They'll keep you moving toward your goals.

I once suggested that a mentee—someone eager to rise into the senior editorial ranks at a magazine—should volunteer to lead a special project. He would need to work with the art director to create a feature article that told its story graphically rather than mainly with text. He took to the assignment with gusto and executed it so well that such projects expanded his portfolio of skills, eventually helping him land the opportunity he was seeking.

FORMAL MENTORING PROGRAMS

Even if you've acquired effective mentoring on your own, there's still much to gain from a formal program. Does your company lack an in-house offering? Try an external one. Career-development consultancies and professional associations are great places to look for mentoring that fits your industry and job function.

Just ask Michael Kohlman, an IT executive for The Cook Group, a highly entrepreneurial medical technology company. With its strong culture of self-reliance, Cook offers no formal leadership-training programs; it regards mentoring as an exotic frill. So Kohlman has found his mentoring elsewhere.

He describes "almost a classic journalistic technique" for seeking leadership guidance: "reaching out to people, doing research," and doing a great deal of reading. "Peter Drucker, Tom Peters—I ate all that stuff up during my formative years," he says. "I was mostly self-taught, with a limited budget." He also cultivated informal relationships with senior executives.

As valuable as all that networking and research was, Kohlman didn't think it was enough. Four years ago, he became a member of the CIO Executive Council, a leadership-development organization for IT executives that's run by the publishers of CIO magazine (my former employer). Among the Council's offerings is Pathways, a program that provides group and individual mentoring. Kohlman signed up.

The IT profession is well stocked with people who have far more responsibility than authority. Since they can't do things by fiat, they have to be persuasive and consultative. Kohlman—soon to be in the thick of implementing a new IT architecture designed to tie together all of Cook's far-flung business units and regions—felt he needed to fortify his selling skills to pull that off. Through a series of group mentoring sessions, Pathways helped Kohlman increase his powers of persuasion.

The group aspect—about which he was initially apprehensive—had a natural multiplier effect. Each group in Pathways has about a half-dozen mentees, led by a single mentor. Because all the members are natives of the IT profession, they understand such defining conditions as the responsibility-without-authority problem. All of them share the need to be a world-class persuader.

"Making a project happen is far more likely when you get people involved and enthused than when it's a mandate," says Kohlman. "Group mentoring gave me the chance to see the approaches others had tried. Having a group to use as a sounding board can be invaluable—especially when that group has no personal stake in the internal influences of your organization."

As much as he credits Pathways with helping him meet his goals, Kohlman is planning to leave the program: "It has nothing to do with its quality," he says,

(continued)

(continued)

"and everything to do with my progress in it." In the past year he has brought two of his direct reports into Pathways. And he now finds himself acting more often as a mentor to others.

He hopes to establish a Pathways-like program at Cook—specifically within the Global IT Management Group. The company has made great strides in reengineering its IT infrastructure to unify its many divisions around the world. But success brings challenges. "We need to develop leaders who will be able to grow with the organization," Kohlman says. He sees mentoring as an indispensable tool for "creating a culture of continual leadership development."

Acknowledging the company's skepticism about formal career development, he says, "I know I'm looking at an uphill battle." Fortunately, the battle will demand the same selling skills that Pathways helped him enhance.

Moving on

As noted earlier, most mentoring relationships have a natural end. After you've achieved your goals, move on before the law of diminishing returns kicks in.

Of course, that doesn't mean you should cut all ties. As the mentoring process winds down, your mentor may become a sponsor who advocates for your advancement in the company. Such rewards should be reciprocated. Perhaps your mentor has drawn fresh ideas, understanding, and inspiration from her exposure to you—the business's next generation. That's a good reason not to be stingy with your comments on what you find strange, perplexing, or exciting about the way your organization works. They may create a lasting—and useful—impression.

Looking back over my suggestions, I can see two things quite clearly. First, effective mentoring requires hard work and commitment from mentees and mentors alike. Second, I would have been far smarter and better served to go for it rather than hang back when I needed this kind of support.

As it happened, my magazine launched as scheduled. It won some editorial awards, and it had an exciting two-year run—before it was cut short by dwindling ad sales. Maybe if I'd gotten guidance from a mentor with commercial chops, things would have turned out differently. For one thing, had I enlisted the mentor I'd identified, I am sure he would have advised me to give up the publisher title—in retrospect it was a distraction—and instead use my editorial skills to boost the magazine's business prospects. Later in my career, I learned a lot about how editors add value to the sales process. I am certain that mentoring would have shortened my learning curve.

Plus, I would have developed an important new skill: asking for help and then making the most of it.

———————

Lew McCreary is an editorial consultant and a contributing editor to HBR. He has launched five magazines over the course of his career and served as a formal and informal mentor to numerous colleagues.

Chapter 9
How to Get More from Your Mentors

by Jodi Glickman

A senior publishing executive at William Morris once told me how baffled she was when an aspiring literary agent asked her to be a mentor. She looked at me and said, "She's got to make me *want* to be her mentor. Isn't she supposed to do something for me?" The answer is a definitive yes.

Mentors can provide valuable insight into your organization, inside information about the politics of the place, and useful over-the-shoulder advice about which people to work with and which ones to avoid. But to get all that and more, you've got to figure out how to repay the favor and make the relationship work for both of you.

We're all busy. Like you, your mentors have competing demands on their time and resources. They might let

Adapted from content posted on hbr.org on September 23, 2009 mentoring fall by the wayside when they're closing a deal, bringing a new product to market, or putting out a fire for an important client. That's why you, as the mentee, must make your mentors' investment in you worth their time and energy.

Here are four ways to provide value to your mentors—and receive more in return.

1. **Keep their interests on your radar so you can share relevant ideas and articles or provide access to resources.** Talia, a coaching client of mine, knew her mentor Fred was keen to create a diverse workplace in the male-dominated financial industry. (Names in this article are disguised.) Shortly after she had interned at his investment management firm as a college student, she decided to pursue a career in an entirely different field—but she still valued his feedback and advice, so she kept the mentoring relationship going. In return for Fred's ongoing guidance, Talia looked for ways to help him recruit female talent. She promoted his firm to her career center on campus and referred potential interns to him. She also introduced him to various women's groups at her university and sent him articles and blog posts about why women were—or weren't—seeking financial jobs. Fred appreciated the introductions and the market intelligence, and continued to counsel Talia on positioning herself and speaking to her skill set as she carved out her new career path. He even tapped his network and

put her in touch with several people in her new industry of choice.

2. **Provide insight into the rank and file of your organization.** Your mentor may feel out of touch with the cubicle culture, as leaders often do. You can help by sharing your peers' reactions to new social-media restrictions at the office, for example. Or, like Margot, a nonprofit program manager, you can explain that your fellow employees have been wanting a flextime policy for ages and offer yourself up as an organizational experiment. Margot's boss and mentor, Bruce, lobbied for her flextime arrangement (the organization's first) and had real skin in the game: If Margot's performance suffered as a result of her working at home one day a week, so would his reputation. But the experiment went well, and Bruce asked Margot to put together a proposal on his behalf for a firm-wide flextime policy. Bruce earned points with colleagues for being forward-thinking and became known as an accommodating (and desirable) boss. He also benefited from Margot's continued loyalty: She was always willing to put in extra time and energy whenever he needed help moving something new through the organization.

3. **Participate in activities and programs your mentor cares about.** Perhaps one of your mentors does a lot of college recruiting for your firm and runs a leadership development program. Why

not offer to accompany her on a recruiting trip or suggest speakers for her leadership program? Consider Caroline, a magazine copy editor who took a special interest in her mentor's "lunch and learn" series, a lineup of informal lectures by guest experts from various fields. Caroline made a point of flagging speakers who were in town for her own alumni events and took the initiative to book several of them for the brown-bag series. Soon her mentor turned the entire series over to her—and Caroline received high marks on her performance review for helping to promote learning in the organization.

4. **Buy 'em lunch.** At the very least, if you really struggle to find ways to add value, take your mentors to lunch or dinner (one at a time, of course). Even if they try to foot the bill, be firm and generous in your offer. Let them know that you appreciate their help and it's your pleasure to be able to return the favor in some small way. A nice glass of wine and a good meal goes a long way toward building goodwill.

———

Jodi Glickman, founder and president of the communication training firm Great on the Job, is the author of *Great on the Job* (St. Martin's, 2011).

Chapter 10
Employ a Personal Board of Directors

by Priscilla Claman

Like avocado-colored appliances, traditional mentoring is something you don't see much anymore. Yes, corporate-sponsored mentoring programs will always improve personal exposure and connections. But the career strategy of hitching your future to some rising manager is outdated.

That's partly because midlevel and senior managers are no longer the ones with stable jobs. Many organizations are dealing with restructuring, downsizing, acquisitions, mergers, and, of course, recessions—so your mentor is just as likely to move on or be laid off as you are. And if you are considered her special protégé, you may lose your job when she does.

Adapted from content posted on hbr.org on October 20, 2010

Another reason one mentor alone won't cut it is that no single person can possibly give you all the guidance and nurturing you'll need to reach your potential. Even the wisest, most insightful people have blind spots, and even the most loyal and committed mentors can offer you only so much of their energy and time.

What you need instead is a board of directors for your career, a group of people you consult regularly to get advice and feedback on matters ranging from job performance to career advancement to personal enrichment. There's no need to hold meetings or even inform each person of his or her status as a board member—but you do need to select the right people, stay in touch, and reciprocate their generosity.

Just like any good board, the people you choose should make different contributions to your thinking about how to reach your professional and personal goals. You might want to include your boss or a colleague you admire—or both. If you are a senior manager, consider job search professionals, academics, and consultants with expertise in your specialty. The people on your board should know more than you about something, be better than you at something, or offer different points of view. Putting only buddies on your board won't help you grow and develop.

Worried that assembling your board will take too much time away from your work? It's actually not all that time-consuming—and your board will help you do your job better and more efficiently, especially if you've been placed in a role before you're fully equipped to handle it. The key is to match up your weaknesses with others' strengths—and, so you can give as well as get, your strengths with their weaknesses.

For example, I often go to my friend Ted, an expert in the world of finance, with questions like "What do the Basel Accords really mean?" and "Why did my corporate client's stock shoot up?" (Names in this article have been changed.) He is full of statistical information, but when he is looking for some up-to-date hunches, like what I think is going on in the job market, he calls me.

I get in touch with Kerry, a former colleague of mine who has a gift for delivering bad news, when I have something particularly difficult to communicate. For instance, Kerry helped me come up with an effective way to tell an upset client why I thought his employer wasn't giving him the promotion he thought he deserved. Kerry turns to me when he has a hard job to fill and wants some leads.

Pat, a longtime client of mine, goes to all the conferences in our field, and she always knows the latest theories and research, so I check in with her periodically to find out what's new. She introduced me to concepts in emotional intelligence and neuroscience long before they became trends. And because she knows I enjoy batting around training ideas, she asks me for suggestions when she's looking for a creative new training exercise.

I have learned from each of these folks. They know I think highly of their advice, and I do what I can to help them in return.

Mentoring from a personal board is also invaluable if you're making a career transition. Ellen, another client of mine, took six years off from a demanding technology career to raise her children. When she was ready to return to work full time, she looked for advice on how to make the transition. She sought out a former colleague, and he was candid: Her technical skills just weren't up-to-date. With his assistance, Ellen identified the new software she needed to know and took a training class. When she asked for extra help in the class, the instructor found her a software coach, and the coach got her connected with a user group. Then, the user group connected her with a headhunter, who told her he could find her a job if she were certified in the software. While working toward the certification, Ellen regularly stays in touch with her former colleague, the instructor, her software coach, and the headhunter to make sure she is on track.

No single mentor could have made the contributions to Ellen's career that all these individuals did. Finding and tapping her personal board members required some elbow grease, but it paid off.

Go forth and consult your own network. Instead of relying on a single upper-level manager, assemble a team of specialists for yourself as if you were creating a company's board of directors. Their combined efforts could yield real results for you.

Priscilla Claman is the president of Career Strategies, a Boston-based firm offering coaching to individuals and career management services to organizations. She is a former corporate human resources executive and the author of *Ask . . . How to Get What You Want and Need at Work* (Insights, 2002).

Chapter 11
A Smarter Way to Network

by Rob Cross and Robert Thomas

One of the happiest, most successful executives we know is a woman named Deb. She works at a major technology company and runs a global business unit that has more than 7,000 employees. When you ask her how she rose to the top and why she enjoys her job, her answer is simple: people. She points to her boss, the CEO, a mentor who "always has her back"; Steve, the head of a complementary business, with whom she has monthly brainstorming lunches and occasional gripe sessions; and Tom, a protégé to whom she has delegated responsibility for a large portion of her division. Outside the company, Deb's circle includes her counterparts in three strategic partnerships, who inspire her with new ideas; Sheila, a

Reprinted from *Harvard Business Review*, July–August 2011 (product #R1107P)

former colleague, now in a different industry, who gives her candid feedback; and her husband, Bob, an executive at a philanthropic organization. She also has close relationships with her fellow volunteers in a program for at-risk high school students and the members of her tennis group and book club.

This is Deb's social network (the real-world kind, not the virtual kind), and it has helped her career a lot. But not because the group is large or full of high-powered contacts. Her network is effective because it both supports and challenges her. Deb's relationships help her gain influence, broaden her expertise, learn new skills, and find purpose and balance. Deb values and nurtures them. "Make friends so that you have friends when you need friends" is her motto.

"My current role is really a product of a relationship I formed over a decade ago that came back to me at the right time," she explains. "People may chalk it up to luck, but I think more often than not luck happens through networks where people give first and are authentic in all they do."

Over the past 15 years, we've worked with many executives like Deb, at more than 300 companies. What began as organizational research—helping management teams understand and capitalize on the formal and informal social networks of their employees—has since metamorphosed into personal programs, which teach individual executives to increase their effectiveness by leveraging their networks.

The old adage "It's not what you know, it's who you know" is true. But it's more nuanced than that. In spite of what most self-help books say, network size doesn't usually matter. In fact, we've found that individuals who simply know a lot of people are less likely to achieve standout performance, because they're spread too thin. Political animals with lots of connections to corporate and industry leaders don't win the day, either. Yes, it's important to know powerful people, but if they account for too much of your network, your peers and subordinates often perceive you to be overly self-interested, and you may lose support as a result.

The data we've collected point to a different model for networking. The executives who consistently rank in the top 20% of their companies in both performance and well-being have diverse but select networks like Deb's—made up of high-quality relationships with people who come from several different spheres and from up and down the corporate hierarchy. These high performers, we have found, tap into six critical kinds of connections, which enhance their careers and lives in a variety of ways.

Through our work advising individual managers, we've also identified a four-step process that will help any executive develop this kind of network. But first, let's take a look at some common networking mistakes.

Getting It Wrong

Many people take a misguided approach to networking. They go astray by building imbalanced networks, pursuing the wrong kind of relationships, or leveraging relationships ineffectively. (See the sidebar "Are You Networking Impaired?") These people might remain successful for a time, but often they will hit a plateau or

ARE YOU NETWORKING IMPAIRED?

In our work, we have identified six common managerial types who get stuck in three kinds of network traps. Do any of the following descriptions fit you?

The wrong structure

- *The formalist* focuses too heavily on his company's official hierarchy, missing out on the efficiencies and opportunities that come from informal connections.

- *The overloaded manager* has so much contact with colleagues and external ties that she becomes a bottleneck to progress and burns herself out.

The wrong relationships

- *The disconnected expert* sticks with people who keep him focused on safe, existing

see their career derailed because their networks couldn't prompt or support a critical transition.

Consider Dan, the chief information officer of one of the world's largest life-sciences organizations. He was under constant pressure to find new technologies that would spur innovation and speed the drug commercialization process at his company, and he needed a network competencies, rather than those who push him to build new skills.

- *The biased leader* relies on advisers much like herself (same functional background, location, or values), who reinforce her biases, when she should instead seek outsiders to prompt more fully informed decisions.

The wrong behavior

- *The superficial networker* engages in surface-level interaction with as many people as possible, mistakenly believing that a bigger network is a better one.

- *The chameleon* changes his interests, values, and personality to match those of whatever subgroup is his audience, and winds up being disconnected from every group.

that would help him. Unfortunately, more than 70% of his trusted advisers were in the unit he had worked in before becoming CIO. Not only did they reinforce his bias toward certain solutions and vendors, but they lacked the outside knowledge he needed. "I had started to mistake friendship, trust, and accessibility for real expertise in new domains," he told us. "This didn't mean I was going to dump these people, as they played important roles for me in other ways. But I needed to be more targeted in who I let influence my thinking."

Another overarching mistake we often see in executives' networks is an imbalance between connections that promote career advancement and those that promote engagement and satisfaction. Numerous studies have shown that happier executives are higher-performing ones.

Take Tim, the director of a large practice area at a leading professional services firm. On the surface he was doing well, but job stress had taken its toll. He was 40 pounds overweight, with alarmingly high cholesterol and blood sugar levels, and prone to extreme mood swings. When things went well at work, he was happy; when they didn't, he wasn't pleasant to be around. In fact, Tim's wife finally broke down and told him she thought he had become a career-obsessed jerk and needed to get other interests. With her encouragement, he joined Habitat for Humanity and started rowing with their daughter. As a result, his social network expanded to include people with different perspectives and values, who helped him focus on more healthful and fulfilling pursuits. "As I spent more time with different groups, what I cared about diversified," he says. "Physically, I'm in much better shape and probably staved off a heart attack. But I think I'm a better leader, too, in that I think about problems more broadly, and I'm more resilient. Our peer feedback systems are also clearly indicating that people are more committed to the new me."

Getting It Right

To understand more about what makes an effective network, let's look again at Deb. She has a small set of core contacts—14 people she really relies on. Effective core networks typically range in size from 12 to 18 people. But what really matters is structure: Core connections must bridge smaller, more-diverse kinds of groups and cross hierarchical, organizational, functional, and geographic lines. Core relationships should result in more learning, less bias in decision making, and greater personal growth and balance. The people in your inner circle should also model positive behaviors, because if those around you are enthusiastic, authentic, and generous, you will be, too.

More specifically, our data show that high performers have strong ties to

1. people who offer them new information or expertise, including internal or external clients, who increase their market awareness; peers in other functions, divisions, or geographies, who share best practices; and contacts in other industries, who inspire innovation;

2. formally powerful people, who provide mentoring, sense-making, political support, and resources; and informally powerful people, who offer influence, help coordinating projects, and support among the rank and file; and

3. people who give them developmental feedback, challenge their decisions, and push them to be

better. At an early career stage, an employee might get this from a boss or customers; later, it tends to come from coaches, trusted colleagues, or a spouse.

Meanwhile, the most satisfied executives have ties to

1. people who provide personal support, such as colleagues who help them get back on track when they're having a bad day or friends with whom they can just be themselves;

2. people who add a sense of purpose or worth, such as bosses and customers who validate their work, and family members and other stakeholders who show them work has a broader meaning; and

3. people who promote their work/life balance, holding them accountable for activities that improve their physical health (such as sports), mental engagement (such as hobbies or educational classes), or spiritual well-being (music, religion, art, or volunteer work).

How does one create such a varied network? We recommend a four-point action plan: analyze, de-layer, diversify, and capitalize.

Analyze

Start by looking at the individuals in your network. Where are they located—are they within your team, your unit, or your company, or outside your organization?

What benefits do your interactions with them provide? How energizing are those interactions?

The last question is an important one. Energizers bring out the best in everyone around them, and our data show that having them in your network is a strong predictor of success over time. These people aren't necessarily extroverted or charismatic. They're people who always see opportunities, even in challenging situations, and create room for others to meaningfully contribute. Good energizers are trustworthy and committed to principles larger than their self-interest, and they enjoy other people. "De-energizers," by contrast, are quick to point out obstacles, critique people rather than ideas, are inflexible in their thinking, fail to create opportunities, miss commitments, and don't show concern for others. Unfortunately, energy-sapping interactions have more impact than energizing ones—up to seven times as much, according to one study. And our own research suggests that roughly 90% of anxiety at work is created by 5% of one's network—the people who sap energy.

Next, classify your relationships by the benefits they provide. Generally, benefits fall into one of six basic categories: information, political support and influence, personal development, personal support and energy, a sense of purpose or worth, and work/life balance. It's important to have people who provide each kind of benefit in your network. Categorizing your relationships will give you a clearer idea of whether your network is extending your abilities or keeping you stuck. You'll see where you have holes and redundancies and which people you depend on too much—or not enough.

Let's use Joe, a rising star in an investment bank, as a case study. He had 24 close advisers—on the surface, a more than healthy number. But many of the people he relied on were from his own department and frequently relied on one another. If he eliminated those redundancies, his network shrank to five people. After giving it some thought and observing his peers' networks, he realized he was missing links with several important types of people: colleagues focused on financial offerings outside his own products, who could help him deliver broader financial solutions to customers; coworkers in different geographies—particularly London and Asia—who could enhance his ability to sell to global clients; and board-level relationships at key accounts, who could make client introductions and influence purchasing decisions. His insularity was limiting his options and hurting his chances of promotion to managing director. He realized he would need to focus on cultivating a network rather than allowing it to organically arise from the day-to-day demands of his work.

De-layer

Once you've analyzed your network, you need to make some hard decisions about which relationships to back away from. First, look at eliminating or minimizing contact with people who sap you of energy or promote unhealthful behaviors. You can do this by reshaping your role to avoid them, devoting less time to them, working to change their behavior, or reframing your reactions so that you don't dwell on the interactions.

John, an academic, realized that two university administrators in his network were causing him a great deal of anxiety. This had so soured his view of his school that he was considering leaving. He therefore decided to devote less time to projects and committees that would involve the negative contacts and to avoid dwelling on any sniping comments they subjected him to. Within a year he was much more productive and happy. "By shifting my role and how I reacted to the idiots, I turned a negative situation around," John says. "In hindsight it was an obvious move—rather than leave a place I loved—but emotions can spiral on you in ways you don't recognize."

The next step is to ask yourself which of the six categories have too many people in them. Early-stage leaders, for example, tend to focus too much on information and not enough on personal development and might want to shed some of the contacts who give them the former to make more time for those who give them the latter.

Beyond this, consider which individuals—and types of people as determined by function, hierarchy, or geography—have too much of you, and why. Is the cause structural, in that work procedures require you to be involved? Or is your own behavior causing the imbalance? What can you change to rectify the situation? Too often we see leaders fail because they accept or create too many collaborative demands.

Paul, the head of research in a consumer products company, had a network of almost 70 people just at work. But he got many complaints from people who said they needed greater access to him. His productivity, and his unit's, was suffering. When he analyzed his network, he realized that he was missing "people and initiatives one or two levels out." To address this, he decided to delegate—stepping away from interactions that didn't require his presence and cultivating "go to" stand-ins in certain areas of expertise. He also changed his leadership style from extraordinarily accessible to helpful but more removed, which encouraged subordinates to solve their own problems by connecting with people around him. "As a leader you can find yourself in this bubble of activity where you feel like a lot is happening moving from meeting to meeting," Paul says. "You can actually start to thrive on this in some ways. I had to move past this for us to be effective as a unit and so that I could be more forward-thinking."

Diversify

Now that you've created room in your network, you need to fill it with the right people. Simple tools like work sheets can help you get started. For example, you might make a list of the six categories of relationships and think about colleagues who could fill the holes you have in each. Remember to focus on positive, energetic, selfless people, and be sure to ask people inside and outside your network for recommendations.

You should also think about how you could connect your network to your professional and personal goals. Here's another simple exercise: Write down three specific business results you hope to achieve over the next year (such as doubling sales or winning an Asia-based client) and then list the people (by name or general role) who could help you with them, thanks to their expertise, control over resources, or ability to provide political support. Joe, the investment banker, identified counterparts in the Asian and European operations of his company who had relationships with the clients he was focused on and then scheduled regular calls with them to coordinate efforts. "In a couple of cases this helped me identify opportunities I could pitch proactively. In others it just helped us appear more coordinated when we were competing against other banks," he says. One of the big challenges for Paul, the consumer products executive, was managing a new facility and line of innovation in China. Because none of his trusted advisers had ever even been to that country, he reached out to the head of R&D at a major life-sciences organization that had undertaken a similar effort.

Capitalize

Last, make sure you're using your contacts as effectively as you can. Are there people you rely on in one sphere, such as political support, that you could also use to fill a need in another, such as personal development? Could you get more out of some relationships if you put more energy into them? Our research shows, for instance, that high performers at all levels tend to use their information contacts to gain other benefits, such as new ideas. Reciprocal relationships also tend to be more fruitful; the most successful leaders always look for ways to give more to their contacts.

Alan, a top executive at a global insurance company, realized that although he had a good network, he was still making decisions in relative isolation. He failed to elicit insights from others and, as a result, wasn't making enough progress toward his goals. So he started inviting his more-junior contacts, who were informal opinion leaders in his company, to lunch and asking them open-ended questions. These conversations led him to streamline decision making and uncover innovation deep within the firm's hierarchy. "When I met with one lady, I was stunned at a great new product idea she had been pushing for months," Alan says. "But she hadn't been able to get the right people to listen. I was able to step in and help make things happen. To me the right way to be tapping into people is in this exploratory way—whether it is about strategic insights or just how they think I'm doing on some aspect of my job. That's how I get to new ways of thinking and doing things, and I know it makes me much more effective than people who are smarter than me."

A network constructed using this four-point model will build on itself over time. In due course, it will ensure that the best opportunities, ideas, and talent come your way.

Rob Cross is an associate professor at the University of Virginia's McIntire School of Commerce. **Robert Thomas** is the executive director of the Accenture Institute for High Performance.

Chapter 12
Accelerate Your Development: Tips for Millennials

by Jeanne C. Meister and Karie Willyerd

Many of the 70 million jobs that Baby Boomers will vacate over the next two decades—from the front lines up to senior management—will go to Gen Xers and Millennials (also known as Generation Y). If you're a Millennial (born after 1980), that might mean early career advancement for you, though you'll have lots of competition for those positions: 88 million others in your generation, plus about 50 million Xers, will also be vying for them.

How do you compete for jobs formerly held by people with decades more experience, especially when you're younger than at least a third of the candidates out there? By putting your mentoring and development on a fast track. Don't wait for your company to notice you and groom you. Be bold—and hungry—as you seek out the counsel you need to become a serious contender for one of those roles Boomers are leaving open. These seven tips will help you scour the landscape for the right mentors, persuade them to work with you, and collaborate with them to accelerate your development.

1. **Build a diverse network of mentors to round out your skills and knowledge.** To fill a retiring Boomer's shoes, you'll probably need to broaden and deepen your skill set—and the longer that takes, the more likely you'll be to lose out to someone who's a quicker "study." Got your eye on a position above you that may open up in a year or two? Compare your experience with that of the person currently in the role to see where you have catching up to do—and look for several mentors who can speed up your learning in key areas. For example, consider reaching out to:

   - A senior executive with experience in a country where your company is expanding— perhaps in an emerging market, such as Brazil or Russia. Use this mentoring relationship as an opportunity to develop a global mind-set about the business you're in.

   - A high-performing peer in an adjacent unit or industry. Say you're a health care marketer, and you're struggling to create innovative campaigns. Try connecting with someone who naturally looks at the health care world through an innovator's lens—a medical-product developer, for instance. He may be equally eager to glean your insights into customer needs.

– A midlevel manager in a sector your business serves. Suppose you work at a tech company, and one of your biggest customers is a government agency. An IT manager in that sector can help you understand how agencies think about security, for example, and what impact new regulations will have on the services your company is developing.

Each mentor in your network should have a distinct area of expertise that complements your knowledge. (For more on building a diverse network of mentors, see Priscilla Claman's article, "Employ a Personal Board of Directors," earlier in this guide.)

2. **Select at least one mentor with only a few more years of experience.** Experts may be so far removed from your day-to-day world that they can't articulate good approaches to the kinds of problems you face. If you wanted to learn to play chess, Bobby Fischer wouldn't be the best person to teach you the basics. Same goes for acquiring work-related skills: Ask a senior executive to counsel you on challenges she hasn't tackled in 20 years, and you'll both probably end up frustrated.

As Andi Litz, a Millennial who works in human resources at General Electric, explains, "Those who are only a couple of years senior can . . . relate to our experiences. Their input and advice will be realistic and achievable." Also, she points out, it's often "easier to develop a trusting relationship" with them, because they're more accessible than senior executives.

When Litz moved to Selmer, Tennessee, to take a new job with GE, she reached out to the person she was replacing. "Since he had just left the job for another one at GE," she says, "he was really helpful. We exchanged lots of phone calls, text messages, and instant messages. I'd be on a big call with people from all over the place, and I could IM him to get quick insight on an initiative that came up in the discussion."

If your organization has an affinity group for Millennials, such as a new-hire club or a young leaders' group, start there to find people who have recently walked in your shoes. Or look for groups in your community that sponsor development for young leaders.

3. **Show potential mentors that they can have a big impact with their limited time.** Your potential mentors—Boomers and Xers in particular—may have complex jobs, time commitments outside work, and multiple mentoring requests coming in from other Millennials. So it's important to treat their time as a precious resource. With some

thought and creativity, you can design a mentoring relationship that moves your development along without placing too many demands on the mentor's schedule.

For starters, select a few critical goals to focus on, and identify ways of measuring success. There's nothing more draining for a mentor than a growing list of goals, with no end in sight. Also, consider buddying up with Millennial peers at your company and asking an experienced manager to work with you as a group on a specific skill, such as making a compelling business case for a new product. A mini class on a discrete topic like that is attractive to a busy mentor because it reins in the conversation. It not only gives the mentor bigger bang for buck but also lends you and your Millennial cohort strength in numbers: You gain visibility as a group that pursues professional growth—and your mentor earns a reputation for nurturing young talent.

4. **Use your mentor's preferred method of communication.** As a Millennial, you may rely heavily on Skype, Facebook, LinkedIn, Twitter, and texting to communicate efficiently. These tools accommodate you wherever you are and can help you keep a brisk dialogue going with your mentor— but only if she likes using them, too.

If she prefers interacting with you in face-to-face meetings and over e-mail, then so be it. She's sharing her time and expertise with you.

Make it easy for her to be generous. After you've found a method that works for her and established a comfortable rhythm, you may discover that she's interested in learning more about social media, for example. That would be a good time to offer a crash course on Twitter and see whether she'd like to start using it to supplement your dialogue.

5. **Remember to *listen*.** Your goal is to learn and develop quickly—and rich feedback is a critical part of rapid development. As a young protégé, you may view your mentoring sessions as opportunities to impress someone who has the power to advance your career. But your mentor will be put off if you do more self-promoting than learning. Access to someone with influence is a terrific benefit of mentoring, but you'll gain greater access by putting growth first, showing a little humility, and making it clear that you take your mentor's advice seriously.

So, if he provides feedback on how to make a more succinct, polished customer pitch, don't respond with a knee-jerk "Yes, I knew that already" or "That doesn't really apply to me now." Instead, restate in your own words what your mentor said, to make sure you've got it right, and ask questions to clarify. Mentors will test you by seeing how you respond to feedback, and the better you are at receiving it, the more of it you will get.

6. **Ask what you can do for your mentor.** Look for ways to give rather than always take. As a Millennial, you have digital skills that your mentor may want to pick up, so offer some reverse mentoring: Show her how to sign up for Google Alerts and receive articles on topics of mutual interest. And if you share documents with your mentor—for example, PowerPoint presentations or white papers from industry analysts—teach her how to use a cloud service like Dropbox so you can easily discuss these without having to e-mail them back and forth. She may discover she likes collaborating this way and start doing the same thing with her own team.

7. **End the relationship before it becomes a chore for the mentor.** It's easy to extend mentoring relationships beyond their usefulness. You get into a groove; you enjoy the stimulating conversations; and you've still got lots to learn in a tight time frame. But resist the temptation to wring ever-more value from your mentor.

   Follow the excellent advice of Ryan Healy, a Millennial who cofounded Brazen Careerist, a career website for young professionals: "Be clear about setting goals, and assess whether you have achieved them," he says. "If the answer is yes, it's time to move on and find a new mentor to assist you with another set of goals while continuing to keep in touch with your mentors past and current." Thank your mentor for all the help you've received—and ask permission to use him as a reference when you're scouting for the next one.

———————

Jeanne C. Meister is a partner at Future Workplace, which helps organizations redefine their corporate learning and talent management strategies. **Karie Willyerd** is the chief learning officer at SuccessFactors, a cloud-based-software company. They are the authors of *The 2020 Workplace: How Innovative Companies Attract, Develop, and Keep Tomorrow's Employees Today* (Harper-Business, 2010).

Chapter 13
Mentoring for Gen Xers

by Tamara Erickson

If you're a member of Generation X (born between the early 1960s and the late 1970s), you may worry that Gen Ys (born after 1980) will get all the mentoring love at work, but don't: You're actually in a pretty good position.

For starters, you're armed with more experience, which you can use to attract good mentors. Think of all that experience as a stack of poker chips acquired for being an effective, valuable contributor over the years—chips that you can now cash in to get the specific career advice and support you need.

Your Gen Y colleagues, no matter how "golden," often receive indiscriminant, same-for-all counsel. Like college freshmen, they have to study the core curriculum before they can spend much time concentrating on a major. So they may sit in on group sessions to learn more about the corporation's values and strategies, for example, or receive coaching on writing effective memos. Much of their mentoring is either broad orientation or basic tactical learning. As a result, it covers a wide range of skills and knowledge, and can be hit or miss—more like the rewards from a slot machine than a payout for a poker game well played.

Now that you're well into your thirties or forties, you need mentoring that's tailored to your individual strengths and career goals. And at this point, you've earned it. But don't expect the company or your Baby Boomer bosses to think of it on their own—*you've* got to be the one to make it happen. How? By playing to your strengths, building a network of mentors who can help you achieve your goals, and working with those mentors to optimize your current role.

Playing to Your Strengths

Earlier in your career, it made sense to try a bit of everything and to push yourself to improve in areas of weakness. Though self-improvement is still an admirable goal, now is the time to consolidate your efforts and focus on what you do best. You'll deepen your expertise and, just as important, attract the attention of mentors who can help you grow and advance in your areas of strength. Ask yourself:

"Am I pursuing opportunities at work that demonstrate my strengths?"

Consider Jonathon, a software specialist at a large distribution firm, who had come to realize that his ability to manage projects well set him apart from his colleagues. (All examples in this article are drawn from my research on Gen X.) He began to seek work assignments that allowed him to highlight that skill set. Because he was organized and good at meeting deadlines, he frequently offered to lead projects. Over time, the VP of his company's project management office took note and began to send increasingly challenging opportunities Jonathon's way. To set him up for success, the VP also mentored Jonathon by sharing the tacit knowledge he'd gained over the years—tips for handling negotiations with difficult stakeholders, for example, and ways to access scarce resources.

"Do my external activities reinforce my professional strengths and reputation?"

When you sign up for responsibilities outside work, try to choose ones that build on your expertise. If you're good at managing large projects, consider joining the school building committee in your district. Or if marketing campaigns are your bailiwick, offer to develop one for a local animal shelter.

Susan, a human resource generalist, was fascinated by the strategic issues associated with talent management and realized she wanted to specialize in that area. As part of her career development plan, she volunteered to serve on the long-range strategy committee of a local arts organization. Helping this committee consider the impact a changing workforce would have on the organization gave her strategy-development experience relevant to her field—and a number of stories she could inject into watercooler conversations at work. She posted updates and lessons learned in her profile on the company's social network. Her reputation for big-picture planning spread quickly. Soon her enthusiasm attracted the attention of several senior managers, who were willing to invest time in mentoring such an obviously dedicated individual: They shared their own experiences and best practices with her, gave her assignments that required an innovative look at future trends' implications for the company, critiqued her work on those assignments, and supported her requests for corporate funding for additional education.

Building a Mentoring Network

At this stage in your career, it's critical to broaden your perspective and increase your access to career-advancement opportunities—and you can do both by building and tapping a network of multiple mentors.

Of course, younger employees create networks of contacts, too, but not typically for the kind of mentoring you'll benefit from. Theirs are often designed to help them get necessary information for immediate tasks or guidance on specific challenges, like delivering effective presentations. Given where you are in your career, your networking goal should be much larger than that: to open doors for growth and advancement.

Ben, a specialist in procurement, worked in a corporation that had several strong, decentralized divisions. He had a solid relationship with his department head, but no contacts in other parts of the company. However, by asking his mentor for targeted introductions, he formed a cross-unit network of influential, in-the-know people within the operational functions in multiple divisions. That's how he learned about a plum opportunity to move into a broader operational management role when it came up in another division.

And then there was Laura, a star in sales who had a long-term goal of moving into marketing. She worked with her mentor to understand which aspects of her past experience would be most applicable to marketing roles (her detailed understanding of the distribution channels, for instance)—and then to position herself as a potential marketer in conversations with others in the firm. Her mentor also introduced her to people who coached her on skills she lacked, such as conducting market research. With confidence in her base of experience and exposure to some new skills, Laura made a successful move into a product manager role when the next one opened up.

Start building your mentoring network by creating a personal relationship map. Identify all the people you need to collaborate with in order to do your current job successfully and everyone who might help you achieve your next job or career goal. Ask yourself which of those individuals you need to know better, and leverage your current mentors to form stronger relationships with them. For example, ask existing contacts to provide key introductions, as Ben's and Laura's mentors did, and have them fill you in on people's backgrounds and interests. Work with your mentors to identify issues or projects your target contacts are working on: Maybe you can offer relevant expertise or ideas, or find ways for your team to assist theirs.

Optimizing Your Current Role

Many midcareer challenges you'll face as a Gen Xer are likely to stem from a mismatch between your tried-and-true approaches to work and your changing roles over the course of your career. In your earlier roles, success probably depended on acquiring knowledge, gaining technical proficiency, and working hard to produce whatever your company produced. But now you may be responsible for managing processes, activities, or other people. Or perhaps you've moved into a senior role, where your job is to establish and reinforce the company's values, strategies, policies, and leadership behaviors. Success, in either case, now depends on your ability to create an environment where *other* people can shine.

Making such transitions is tough because knowledge and skills that previously served you well no longer apply. One of the most important roles mentors play at this point in your career is to help you see yourself clearly and modify your behavior appropriately as you strive to meet new expectations. It's difficult to get this perspective yourself—and the kind of honest feedback that's required is not something a casual colleague is likely to provide. You need trusted mentors, invested in helping you succeed.

Take Barbara's situation. Based on her terrific work as a research analyst, she was viewed as a rising star at her company and promoted at a young age to a senior position that involved managing many others. Her new direct reports were also acknowledged stars or eager to become recognized. Barbara's role abruptly shifted from *producing content* as an individual contributor to *creating context* where other contributors could perform well. Fortunately, a mentor helped her adjust her focus and tone—for instance, by doing some role-playing with Barbara to prepare her for difficult types of conversations. From such exercises, Barbara learned that she needed to soften her tone and adopt a more nurturing attitude. Her mentor showed her how to convey genuine respect and caring for her direct reports through word choice and body language, and explained the importance of gaining their trust by acknowledging their accomplishments and their need for recognition.

Mentoring for Gen Xers is a reinforcing circle: The more you use your experience to build your reputation and your network, the easier it will become to attract effective mentors. And by working with those mentors, you can leverage the knowledge and skills honed in your current role to grasp the next big opportunity.

———————

Tamara Erickson works with corporations to more effectively engage the changing workforce. She is the author of a trilogy of books on the generations: *Retire Retirement, Plugged In,* and *What's Next, Gen X?* (Harvard Business Review Press, 2008, 2008, and 2010). She was named one of the 50 leading management thinkers in 2009 and 2011 by Thinkers50

Chapter 14
Keep Learning from Your Protégés

by Hollis Heimbouch

I'm fortunate to work in publishing, a field that has long relied on an apprenticeship model of talent management and promotion. Like many of my peers, I began my career as an editorial assistant, reporting to two senior editors. They were responsible for finding and developing new book projects, which seemed to require many fancy meals and trips to glamorous locales. And I was responsible for handling all the sundry details of getting books out the door, which required lots of trips to the photocopier and the mailroom. (We're talking late 1980s.) A recent college graduate, fresh-faced and naive, I thought I knew a lot about literature—but I knew absolutely nothing about the business of books.

I was mentored well by my two supervisors. They allowed me to sit in on calls with authors, read manuscripts, and contribute feedback. They offered me an unvarnished look into the life of an editor. A few years later I was finally in charge of my own projects and mentoring an editorial assistant of my own—and I learned as much from her as I did from my senior colleagues.

The great thing about working with people who are eager to learn is they aren't afraid to ask questions. Bone-headed questions, profound questions: Why don't we just publish best sellers? Why is one author a dream to work with and another the subject of recurring nightmares? How do I edit a book? How do I judge a good jacket design? How do I say no without burning a bridge? How much is a project "worth"?

I tried to be a good mentor, but I can't lie: At first I resented the amount of time and effort involved, afraid that all the yammering might take me away from "important" editorial work. But the more we talked about what it meant to be an editor and what it was I actually *did*, the more I came to understand the craft myself. In these conversations, I was able to articulate the mental checklist I used to assess a project's merits and inherit risks— financial, psychic, and otherwise. I was able to identify a set of communication techniques, a list of dos and don'ts, that had proven helpful in dealing with difficult authors. And I came to see that my work didn't depend solely on hyper-productivity (the number of projects acquired, the number of best sellers); emotional intelligence and the care and feeding of long-term relationships mattered just as much. Previously these so-called soft skills hadn't much figured into my daily to-do list, but I now realized they were at the heart of what made some editors great.

My assistant's almost total lack of inhibition gave me, the smarty-pants senior editor, a second chance to learn critical, intangible aspects of my job: *why* I did things the way I did and what assumptions were behind my actions. Psychologists call this practice of "thinking about how we think" *metacognition*, and I would argue it lies at the heart of every productive *reverse mentoring* relationship, where the teacher learns from the student.

The first time around, as novices, we learn a lot by doing—by making mistakes, by self-correcting, by having our errors pointed out by others. The second time around we learn by teaching someone else to do what we do. That process forces us to be explicit about the embedded rules and mental models we've been using to make decisions. It reinforces and clarifies what we know in our guts.

It's this second-time-around learning that turns good professionals and managers into great ones. While we're imparting new knowledge and perspectives to our mentees, we're also gaining deeper insight into what we do. In the best of these relationships, it's hard to tell the mentee from the mentor, so symbiotic is the learning and exchange.

The trick is not to get hung up by hubris once you feel you've "arrived." Even the most seasoned of us have much to learn not just by looking up the ladder but also by looking down, around, and even outward, to people in other departments or fields. If you get snooty and dismiss unusual suspects from your lineup of potential mentors, you'll miss out on important guidance and growth. I picked up that lesson the hard way.

As a lifelong runner, I had gotten bored with marathons as I approached my 40th birthday and decided to compete in a triathlon. But I'd never swum competitively, despite having learned basic swimming skills as a kid. So what did I do? I brought the same discipline to swimming that I'd brought to running and, for that matter, editing. I read books, watched videos, and spent several hours a week thrashing through laps on my own and trying to pick up tricks by observing other swimmers. And still I wasn't getting much better. Stubbornly I completed a few triathlons training this way. But when I examined the race results, my swim times consistently put me in the bottom 20% of overall finishers. How could this happen after I'd worked so hard?

At a loss, I spoke to another triathlete, a much better swimmer than I was. She pointed out that swimming is highly technical, more so than running or cycling; much depends on the physics of body position, stroke, and so forth. I'd read as much in my manuals, of course, and tried to follow the instructions, but something was still missing.

Finally I gave up and hired a swim coach, even though I found it galling to take advice from a brawny guy named Coach Mike, whom I could easily outrun in a 10K road race. In the pool, though, he was Baryshnikov. Together we began breaking down my so-called technique, with Coach Mike showing me how poor form and a bevy of tiny errors had caused me to be inefficient in the water. It was tedious work, often involving my performing idiotic-looking drills as other swimmers sliced the water in adjacent lanes. Coach Mike spoke somewhat mystically about learning to "feel" the water, understanding instinctively how it works with and against your body. The metacognition of swimming, if you will.

Even as I longed to experience that "feel," I was amazed at how a shift in the position of my hips or a slightly more bent elbow, for instance, resulted in marked and immediate improvements. I was not only swimming faster but also expending less energy doing so. I could never have made these corrections on my own, no matter how much time I spent in the water or how many DVDs I watched. Even today, swimming is still my weakest sport, but I've graduated from thrashing to "feeling it"—and perhaps more important, I'm now able to recognize when I'm starting to lose that feel so I can refocus on the fundamentals of good form.

Of course, the larger lesson isn't about the need to refine technique or even to hire a coach. It's about how difficult, but necessary, it is to prevent ourselves from becoming atrophied by success and pride. It took me three times longer to become a decent swimmer than it should have because I'd lost the openness and humility that makes learning possible. I'd considered myself proficient in other parts of my life—working, editing, running, being a grown-up in general—and expected the rules I already knew to apply to swimming. I'd brought my ego to the pool, acting with fear and self-consciousness rather than with the inquisitiveness that had served me well early in my professional life.

Mastery can become a closed world; we do only those things that reinforce a positive image of ourselves. By contrast, being a novice can make highly specialized skills seem easy to master: a simple matter of jumping in and flapping around. That's why it's so powerful to bring together the intensity of learning-by-doing with the reflection in learning-by-teaching. It's the reciprocity between the two that leads to satisfaction and growth over the course of a career.

As I head toward my third decade in publishing and my sixth year as a swimmer, I'm trying to stay in close touch with the kids in the world—not just because they can teach me jazzy things about social media and computer games but also because their questions encourage me to keep asking my own.

———————

Hollis Heimbouch is the vice president and publisher of Harper Business, an imprint of HarperCollins, and a former associate publisher/editorial director of Harvard Business Review Press. She continues to compete in road races and triathlons, creaky joints permitting.

Index

Notes

Notes

Notes

Notes